THE
MANY-SIDED
CROSS
OF
JESUS

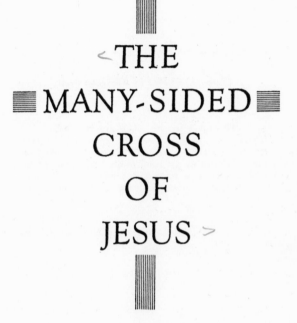

THE
MANY-SIDED
CROSS
OF
JESUS

Alan Walker

Abingdon Press

NEW YORK ● NASHVILLE

THE MANY-SIDED CROSS OF JESUS

Copyright © 1962 by Abingdon Press

Library of Congress Catalog Card Number: 62-7229

SET UP, PRINTED, AND BOUND BY THE
PARTHENON PRESS, AT NASHVILLE,
TENNESSEE, UNITED STATES OF AMERICA

To
Our Son
Christopher

Foreword

THE CROSS OF JESUS IS THE CENTER OF MY RELIGIOUS LIFE
and experience. Ever since, as a boy, I passed through a
decisive evangelical experience of Christ as Saviour my
faith has been based on the death of Jesus at Calvary. Over
the years I have sought increasingly to express that faith.

When invited by W. C. Finch of Southwestern University in Georgetown, Texas, to give the Willson Lectures,
my mind turned at once to the cross of Jesus as a possible
theme. Thus it was that the material in these pages was
first used as the Willson Lectures. So generously were they
received by the faculty and students at Southwestern that
I dare to give them wider currency. Through these pages
I am trying to say to all who may read them the simple
words of an old hymn:

"O, that my Saviour were your Saviour, too."

ALAN WALKER

Contents

CHAPTER I

The Many-Sided Cross

IN A CATHEDRAL IN COPENHAGEN THERE HANGS A FAMOUS painting that depicts the meeting between John the Baptist and Jesus beside the river Jordan. John is speaking to the crowd as Jesus appears, walking toward him down the hill. As John catches sight of Jesus, he points those around him to the Christ. "Behold the Lamb of God, which taketh away the sin of the world!" (John 1:29.)

There is one unusual feature in the picture. It is the way the artist has painted John's upraised, pointing finger. The finger is swollen, elongated. It seems to be shouting the message: "Behold the Lamb of God!"

Since Jesus came, living, dying, and rising again, men have followed that pointing finger and have tried to understand the meaning of him who came to remove the sin of the world. Christians have come to recognize that the greatest single event in all history is the death of Jesus of Nazareth. We know now that we learn more of man and more of God through the cross of Jesus, as the climax to his life, than anywhere else.

In the earliest days of the church the burden of the Christian preacher's message was: "Christ died for our sins." Paul, as he journeyed through the ancient world, cried with unrestrained passion: "But God forbid that I should glory, save in the cross of our Lord Jesus Christ" (Gal. 6:14). In every generation men and women have humbly bowed at the foot of the cross, gratefully appropriating "the benefits of his passion." Christian thinkers have from the beginning grappled with the mystery of the death of Jesus and have sought to understand its meaning for man.

To move through the history of Christian experience and thought upon the cross of Jesus is to be immersed in the most profound intellectual undertaking of all time. In generation after generation, century after century, men have looked up from the foot of the cross and have tried to understand it. Fascinated, awed, despairing, they have continued on, grateful to be able to express some flash of insight concerning God's greatest encounter with man.

In turning toward the cross of Jesus, the mood of John Milton overtakes us. Milton once wrote an exquisite poem on the birth of Jesus and entitled it, "An Ode on the Morning of Christ's Nativity." He planned a companion poem on the death of Jesus. Only a few lines were written and have come down to us. With them is the significant comment: "This subject the author finding to be above the years he had when he wrote it, and nothing satisfied with what was begun, left it unfinished."

As we dare to grapple again with the meaning of the death of Jesus, I want to make a simple claim. The cross of Jesus is a many-sided cross. No insight, no doctrine, no school of thought can possibly express the whole truth of God revealed in the death of his Son. All bring some partial insight into its meaning. The more angles from which we can view the Cross, the more adequately shall we penetrate the mystery of it.

Let me put it this way. A diamond can be taken and held aloft. As it is slowly turned about in the hand, light flashes, with varying colors, from its many facets. Beauties are seen in the diamond, by looking at it from different angles, that otherwise would remain undiscovered. So it is with the cross of Jesus. To take one explanation of God's reconciling act in Jesus is to limit his cross. Hence we must look together at the Cross in varying ways. As we hold it aloft the wonder of it all will come to some of us in one way; to others, in another. From some facet of its meaning, God's saving act could reach our hearts and transform our lives.

It is significant that the Christian church has never defined and proclaimed an official, orthodox doctrine of the Atonement, as it has done with other aspects of Christian truth. Usually, after decades or centuries of Christian thought, the day has come when a doctrine has been formulated, and it then becomes the accepted view of the church.

Take the doctrine of the Person of Christ as an example.

For at least three centuries a mighty debate proceeded. Was Christ man or God? Then came the period of the great councils of the church. Out of them came the Apostles' and Nicene creeds, clearly defining what has become the accepted, orthodox doctrine of the Person of Christ.

There is no orthodox theory of the Atonement. In the historic creeds of the church the only reference to Christ's death is in the phrase "crucified under Pontius Pilate." By this attitude the Christian church has said—led surely by the Holy Spirit—that no explanation of the death of Christ, no doctrine of the Cross is sufficient in itself to be regarded as the whole truth.

We are virtually invited by the church to hold aloft the cross of Jesus and to contemplate it in thought and devotion, seeking its many meanings. And this is what Christians have always done. In New Testament days and since, men have grappled with its mystery, expressing such truth as they could see in the terms of their personal and cultural experience.

The great British theologian, Vincent Taylor, has written a notable trilogy of books on the Atonement.[1] With painstaking scholarship he has examined the New Testament, and particularly the four Gospels, in an effort to discover the interpretations of the cross of Jesus to be found there. He comes to the conclusion—and I think proves his point—that the cross of Jesus as seen in the New Testament itself is a many-sided cross. He details no less than fourteen ideas or rudimentary theories of the

[1] *Jesus and His Sacrifice, The Atonement in New Testament Teaching, Forgiveness and Reconciliation.*

Atonement in the New Testament. He lists them as follows:

The necessity of Christ's death or its place in the Divine intention, its Messianic character, its voluntary and vicarious nature, its representative aspect, its relation to sin, its sacrificial significance, its connection with the Servant-conception, its association with the resurrection or with the thought of a Living and ascended Lord, the presence of the ideas of a faith-relationship between the believer and the Crucified, the development of eucharistic teaching in connection with the Christ's self-offering, the idea of sharing His sufferings, the thought of His death as a proof or revelation of the love of God.

Dr. Taylor then adds: "All these ideas, to a greater or lesser degree, we are able to trace, although in the case of some of them the signs are faint indeed." [2]

As might be expected, with the authority the Bible always has for Christians, all fourteen glimpses of the meaning of the Cross in the New Testament have been developed by one or another theologian in the long story of Christian thought. The history of thought on the Atonement is as varied as the thought of the New Testament itself. In other words, the Christian church has always presented to the world a many-sided cross of Jesus.

One fact deserves early emphasis. It is that the thought forms and cultural experiences of varying historic periods have exerted a powerful influence on the theories of the Atonement advanced over the last two thousand years.

[2] *The Atonement in New Testament Teaching* (London: The Epworth Press), p. 71.

Thus, in days when the Jewish sacrificial system or slavery or feudalism or forensic ideas dominated men's minds and experience, the Cross was understood in these terms. This was inevitable and right. By such relevance of word and metaphor truth reached the people.

A warning needs to be sounded, however. Ideas, interpretations should not be retained when the period which has given them birth passes away. Otherwise, a metaphor, a doctrinal expression of truth, no longer conveys anything real and vital to those in another period who hear it. This fact also obliges Christian thinkers in every cultural period to struggle to remint truth in thought forms which are meaningful for their own time.

Before seeking to understand some of the insights of the New Testament and of the past, and before attempting some reinterpretation of the many-sided Cross, there are some general principles which must be stated. There are truths which should remain points of reference in every phase of thinking upon the death of Jesus. If we neglect these fundamental truths we shall surely lose our way.

A first towering principle to be remembered in every attempted interpretation of the Cross is that any explanation of the death of Jesus must honor God. The Cross is God's mighty act. Therefore, no theory, no doctrine must ever drive a wedge between God and his Son Jesus Christ. The Cross must reveal, not distort, the face of God.

There have been many presentations of the death of Jesus which have subtly dishonored God the Father. They have unconsciously surrounded God with ideas of arbitrary ruthlessness and unjust harshness. They have made

God petulant, angry, and mean. As a consequence they have led to the kind of outburst which was once heard from the lips of a little girl: "I love Jesus, but I hate God."

A famous evangelist, in seeking to present substitutionary ideas of the Atonement, was preaching in London. He used the forbidding Tower of London with its record of suffering and execution as an illustration of how God works. He invited his hearers to imagine a man lying in the Tower of London awaiting execution. He described how news came that another had come forward and offered to die in his stead. He said that there would be joy unspeakable in the mind and heart of the one now released as he went free and another died in his place. So, he said, Christ stepped into our condemned place, dying for us; and we go free.

To examine closely such an illustration is to see its dangerous fallacies. What worthy man could be elated with joy when escape means that another innocent man unjustly dies? Even more seriously, what kind of God is it who would send an innocent one, even his own Son, to die unjustly in another's place? Such a story presents a picture of God which is a dark distortion of the God whom Jesus revealed to us as our heavenly Father.

The truth which must be retained under all circumstances is that God is the one who takes the initiative, God is the one who is accomplishing his mighty acts in Christ. Even the great Charles Wesley was led into error in one of his hymns by forgetting this truth. Many Protestants over the last two centuries have sung the words.

> My God is reconciled;
>> His pardoning voice I hear;
> He owns me for His child,
>> I can no longer fear:
> With confidence I now draw nigh,
> And, "Father, Abba, Father," cry.

The error is in that first line. God is not reconciled by the actions of his Son, Jesus Christ; God is the reconciling agency. To this truth we must ever cling, else we dishonor God. As Paul said, with great insight: "God was in Christ, reconciling the world unto himself" (II Cor. 5:19) .

In any interpretation of the Cross, the mind of Jesus is all-important. His attitude to his own death must be determinative. Not Paul, not the later New Testament epistles, not the explication of doctrines of the Atonement by the Church Fathers or later Christian thinkers, nor anything else can take priority over Christ himself. His mind is the final court of appeal.

Jesus accepted the Cross, seeing in it a way of serving God his Father and the only way of saving his people. As he came nearer the end of his life he believed that he could do something by dying that would not be accomplished by longer living. He thus went out to meet death, not in resignation or bitterness, but as one accomplishing a mighty task. It was not the demeanor of one who felt he was merely a victim of evil forces that were crushing him. He accepted the Cross, facing it positively, creatively. As he said: "I lay down my life, that I might take it again. No man taketh it from me, but I lay down of myself.

I have power to lay it down, and I have power to take it again." (John 10:17-18.)

No one can understand the mind of Jesus toward his approaching death who does not go back to the fifty-third chapter of Isaiah. There is every evidence that Jesus pondered for long years over the vision of Isaiah and came to see himself in terms of the fulfillment of the prophecy of Isaiah 53. I imagine that way back in the beginning of his ministry—or even earlier, while at Nazareth—there came a day when he was reading the Book of Isaiah. As he read the fifty-third chapter with its concept of the Suffering Servant, he realized that this was the way he must go. The magnificent sentences penetrated his mind, soaking into his very soul:

> He is despised and rejected of men;
>   a man of sorrows, and acquainted with grief:
> . . . .
> Surely he hath borne our griefs,
>   and carried our sorrows:
> . . . .
> But he was wounded for our transgressions,
>   he was bruised for our iniquities:
> the chastisement of our peace was upon him;
>   and with his stripes we are healed.
> . . . .
> And he bare the sin of many,
>   and made intercession for the transgressors.
>   —*Isa. 53:3, 4, 5, 12*

Cannot you imagine the scene? Perhaps as Jesus read these words in the quiet of the Galilean hills or on the plateau of temptation above Jericho their significance for him became clear. This is the way he must go. In complete and trustful obedience he bowed his head and accepted it all.

As Jesus moved toward the Cross, seeing it loom ever larger before him, he kept steadily to his course. It was not the movement of a man who was blindfolded or helpless but of one who remained Master of events, offering a full response in faith and obedience. So we read in Mark: "It is written of the Son of man, that he must suffer many things." (Mark 9:12.) In the vital sentence of Matt. 20:28 the same conviction is expressed: "The Son of man came not to be ministered unto, but to minister, and to give his life a ransom for many." Christ came to accept and understand his own approaching death. Thus it is to his mind that we must ever go. It supplies vital, conclusive evidence for interpretation. No theory, no doctrine that ignores or does violence to the revelation which we receive from Jesus himself can ever be sustained.

A third principle of interpretation that must be constantly remembered is that the salvation which Christ offers must be seen to come from his whole life and ministry. It is only as we see the birth, the life, the teaching, the death, and the resurrection of Jesus together that we can understand the true nature of his redemption for mankind.

Many grave distortions in Christian thinking have developed because the death of Jesus has been looked at in isolation from the rest of his life. The very phrase used by such theologians as P. T. Forsyth, "the work of Christ," has its unfortunate aspects. It has resulted in the isolation of the Cross.

A Russian writer, Dmitri Merezhkovski, in his book *Jesus the Unknown,* has a striking sentence. He says: "The light shed upon the life of Jesus is so arranged that it resembles a long, narrow, dark room, only at the end of which—the death—all the rays are concentrated in one blinding blaze. The light increases from the beginning of the life to the end . . . brightest of all are the minutes on the cross."

This is a necessary emphasis. How can we understand the climax of Christ's life, which is his death, without moving toward it through the events of his teaching and healing ministry? As Christians who regard the Resurrection as central to faith, how can we interpret the Cross without looking back at it through the resurrection experience?

Let me illustrate. Through the skillful and inspired writings of the leader of the Scott expedition to the South Pole, Captain James Scott himself, we have a very full record of that brave and tragic event. The men who perished in the snow made a tremendous impact upon the people of their day, and their influence lives on still. Yet how little we would have really known of the courage and resourcefulness of men like Captain Scott, Edward Wilson, and their companions had they not passed through the tragic suffering and death which became their lot! Through the writings of Captain Scott we are taken into the lonely freezing tent in the Antarctic and are able to glimpse the spirit of men who knew they were destined to die. Through the crisis that overtook them, we discover the quality of their mind and heart. Death revealed their greatness.

So it is with Jesus. We know a great deal of him because of his teaching and his example. But it is under the impact of the last terrible week of his life and all that happened at Calvary that we come to know him most intimately. Yet the Christ whom we watch on the cross is the same Christ who worked and witnessed in Galilee, in Nazareth and Jerusalem. The impact of the cross is really the impact of the Christ who hangs upon it. We only understand that Christ as we see him in the wholeness of his life, as we move toward the climax of death through the insights we gain of him in the more pleasant and relaxed days of his earlier ministry.

In our own actual experience of the saving power of Christ and our interpretation of it, the "work of Christ" cannot be separated from the life of Christ. All combine to be a cleansing, redeeming experience. The salvation of Christ would be nothing like as complete to us if the only record we had was of the last two days, stretching from his agony in the garden to the triumphant cry, "It is finished," on the cross. It is precisely because this cross is the climax of all that went before that it is so great a force for redemption in our hearts.

There is a hymn which expresses the wholeness of Christ's salvation:

God in Jesus lived for me
Far away in Galilee,
By the bloom of Nazareth,
In the desert's burning breath;
There in matchless radiancy
God in Jesus lived for me.

God in Jesus died for me
On the ridge of Calvary,
Well foreknowing all my blame,
Feeling all my silent shame;
Broken with my misery
God in Jesus died for me.

God in Jesus rose for me
Fair with immortality,
Robed and crowned with endless light,
Girded with celestial might—
High in undreamt majesty
God in Jesus rose for me.

God in Jesus lives for me,
Bears with me most patiently,
Seeking when I go astray
Down each troubled darkened way—
Loving everlastingly
God in Jesus lives for me.[3]

A fourth principle to be held is that at the heart of the cross of Jesus is a tremendous moral and ethical demand. The cross of Jesus is God's mighty redeeming act for us men and for our salvation. It is also a way of life. Its

[3] Nicholas John Cocks.

message is horizontal as well as vertical; it calls us to express in our daily lives the Spirit it reveals.

There has always appeared a type of evangelical experience, based on the cross of Jesus, which has been ethically weak. People have sung with great fervor, "Jesus, keep me near the cross," but that has been all. From a sentimental attachment to the cross of Jesus they have gone out to treat Negroes as less than brothers in Christ and have traded sharpness in business dealings with the unredeemed in the capitalist, competitive struggle.

Pierre Van Paassen tells in his book *Days of Our Years* of an old Dutchman who attempted to commit suicide. He waded out into the ocean, but was rescued before the waters closed over his head. Asked why he was ready to commit the sin of self-destruction he said: "I did it, banking on the blood of Jesus."

An ethical awareness of the way of the cross as a way of life is our need. It must result in a response by faith and obedience if it is to be real. The faith-union between the Spirit of Jesus as supremely expressed in his death and the spirit of the one receiving redemption is fundamental. It is another of the principles which belong to every possible explanation of the many-sided cross of Jesus.

One further principle can be declared. It is that the religious forces which are released into human society and lives like ours from the cross of Jesus come from Christ himself and not from any doctrine or theory of the Atonement. This means that we can be saved through the Cross without intellectually or doctrinally understanding very much of its complexities. It is not through intellectual assent that we are saved, but through the establishment of a faith-union between Christ and ourselves that his power flows upon us. Paul went through the ancient world saying simply: "Christ died for our sins according to the scriptures" (I Cor. 15:3). As men accepted this great affirmation, as they bowed before the cross, humbled by the Spirit of the Christ who was dying there, his power stole into their hearts. It is still so today. Any man, any woman who says simply, "Christ died for me," without understanding all of how it happened, can find Christ's redemption.

It is a simple yet necessary fact to remember that experience always precedes doctrine and intellectual explanation. Any interpretation of the Cross, any theory of the Atonement only has significance as it is preceded by somebody's experience. Because of this fact it is the experience that matters. The effort must ever go on, intellectually, to formulate an understanding of what takes place. But the salvation is not in the theory, it is not in theology; it is in the Christ, in his spirit, in the totality of his impact upon us, in the love that is released into our hearts through the contemplation of his death.

There is a vivid illustration of this truth at Calvary itself. Hanging on the cross beside Jesus was one whom we have come to know as "the Dying Thief." He obviously could have known very little about Jesus and certainly had scarcely any insight as to what was happening on the central cross beside him. Something, however, reached his spirit. Turning his face toward the Christ he said: "Lord, remember me when thou comest into thy kingdom." Jesus looked toward him, and for a moment we can imagine a smile chasing away the pain from his face. Quietly he spoke the words of hope: "Verily I say unto thee, To day shalt thou be with me in Paradise." (Luke 23:42, 43.) The meaning now is that at that instant salvation came to the one who had groped toward the Christ. The "Dying Thief" had no understanding, intellectually, of what Jesus was doing by dying at his side. Not even a rudimentary doctrine of Atonement could have been in his mind. He could, however, be touched with the greatness and the love and the power of the Christ at his side. He could bow in humility before the One who was near him. And this he did. As he there bowed his spirit before the Christ he received the gift of redemption.

In the early experience of the church similar happenings of receiving salvation were frequent. In the sixteenth chapter of the Acts of the Apostles is the story of the conversion of the Philippian jailer. Under the impact of the witness of Paul and Silas he asks a simple question: "Sirs, what must I do to be saved? And they said, Believe on the Lord Jesus Christ, and thou shalt be saved, and thy house." (Acts 16:30-31.)

Vincent Taylor says: "The simplest form of faith in Christ contains within itself the germ and the potency of its fullest development. That is why the simplest appeal of the evangelist may prove to be the beginning of the Christian experience." [4]

[4] *The Cross of Christ.* Used by permission of the publishers, Macmillan & Co., Ltd., London; St. Martin's Press, Inc., New York; and The Macmillan Company of Canada Limited.

It is the experience which can come to us all. If we are willing humbly to bow before the cross of Jesus, salvation can reach us. The simple confession of faith is enough: "Jesus died for me." Later we must attempt to explain what has happened to us. We must go on in the long, unending struggle to find a reason for the faith that has been born in us. We must battle for an adequate intellectual presentation of the meaning of the life and death and resurrection of Jesus so that others may be confronted with it all. Something can and must happen before this moment is reached. That something is the acceptance of the Christ who died for us. "Christ died for our sins according to the scriptures."

One day the meaning of words such as these came home to me. I was reading the claim of Jesus: "And I, if I be lifted up from the earth, will draw all men unto me" (John 12:32). Suddenly it all seemed so clear. Lift him up, the Holy Spirit seemed to say. Stand beneath his cross in humble contemplation. To meditate on his sacrifice is to set its wonder flowing into our hearts. Lift him up in thought and imagination and the miracle happens. Lift him up!

Chapter II

The Unchanging Love of God

IN THE TWELFTH CENTURY THERE LIVED A CHRISTIAN THINK-er whose name was Peter Abelard. Abelard was born in 1079, and early showed great powers of intellect. By the time he reached his early twenties he was a force to be reckoned with in Paris. Crowds flocked to hear his lectures and sermons. In the year 1115 Abelard was made a canon of Notre Dame Cathedral, and he enjoyed a popularity in Paris such as no lecturer or speaker had ever enjoyed.

While ministering at Notre Dame Cathedral, Abelard fell in love with Héloïse, a woman of singular devotion and beauty of character who was a niece of a fellow canon of the Cathedral, a man named Fulbert. After a child was born to them, Héloïse and Abelard entered into a secret marriage. Then tragedy struck at them. Her uncle, Canon

Fulbert, believing Abelard was about to abandon his niece, had Abelard waylaid and emasculated.

Abelard, suffering from this terrible mutilation, became separated from Héloïse, and because of the scandal was debarred from advancement in the church. Leaving Notre Dame he became a monk; however, teaching was his life and soon he was lecturing again. His views, contrary to the orthodoxy of the day, were soon attacked by his enemies, and his theories were actually condemned at a synod in Soissons, France in 1121. His life continued to be stormy. He was forced into obscurity, from which he continued to emerge from time to time, always commanding a following because of the attractiveness and strength of his views.

Héloïse herself was crushed by the tragedy that had overtaken the man she loved. She retired into a little nunnery, and in time she became its head. She and Abelard wrote to each other constantly and their letters, which have come down to us, make one of the loveliest records of tender affection which have emerged from the Middle Ages.

Bernard of Clairvaux, a powerful religious leader of the age, maintained his persecution of Abelard, and was able to procure his condemnation as a heretic at the synod of Sens in 1141. Abelard fought back and appealed to Pope Innocent II, but his appeal was rejected. Being condemned for his views by the pope, Abelard became broken in spirit. Under all the pressure and condemnation he actually recanted, denying his convictions, and accepted submission to the power of the pope. Abelard did not live long after his condemnation and in 1142 died in one of the monasteries conducted by the Abbot of Cluny.

Abelard's name is forever associated with what is known as the Moral Influence theory of the Atonement. He was the first to give clear expression to ideas which have persisted and been re-expressed in every period of Christian thought. His influence remains massive wherever men struggle to understand the many-sided cross of Jesus.

Unfortunately, the theological writings of Abelard which have come down to us are all too meager. One of the seemingly most valuable, "An Introduction to Theology," has perished; however, his "Commentary on the Romans," which contains his teachings on the Atonement, has been preserved.

Abelard's conviction, in its simplest forms, is that the cross of Jesus supremely shows the love of God and that this love calls forth an answering love in human hearts. This answering love is a saving, transforming experience which brings about a return to God. God, because of his great love, accepts the one who returns and reconciliation is complete.

Let me quote Abelard's own words:

How cruel and unjust it appears that any one should have demanded the blood of the innocent as any kind of ransom. . . . It seems to us, however, that we are justified by the blood of Christ and reconciled to God in the following way. His Son took our nature and persevered in instructing us both in word and deed even unto death. This was the singular grace shown us through which He more abundantly bound us to Himself by love; so that, set on fire as we are by so great a benefit from the Divine Grace, true charity should fear nothing at all." [1]

Perhaps it is in a beautiful hymn, written by Abelard himself, that we grasp the clearest insight into his interpretation of the Cross.

> Alone Thou goest forth, O Lord
> In sacrifice to die;
> Is this Thy sorrow nought to us
> Who pass unheeding by?
>
> Our sins, not thine, Thou bearest, Lord,
> Make us Thy sorrow feel,
> Till through our pity and our shame,
> Love answers Love's appeal.

It was a man who had stood at the foot of the cross of Jesus who wrote the words: "God is love" (I John 4:8). All Christian thinkers, whatever their theories, accept the fact that the cross of Jesus reveals the love of God. It is the fundamental meaning which the New Testament gives to the Cross: "God so loved the world, that he gave his only begotten Son, that whosoever believeth in him should not perish, but have everlasting life" (John 3:16).

What, then, is the nature of God's love? God's love is a universal love, encompassing the whole created universe. Nothing, nobody lives beyond the range of that love.

God loves the universe he has made. As an artist loves his painting, an author his book, an architect his building,

---

[1] From Abelard's *Commentary on Romans.*

so God loves everything his creative power has brought into being.

God's love reaches to the whole world of people. None can outstrip his tender care. The best of men, the worst of men, are held constantly in his love. During the life of Jesus outcasts and sinners were amazed to find Jesus at their side. It is still true. We may name the men whom we imagine as the least attractive, perhaps the most wicked, of those around us—extortioners, prostitutes, murderers, communists. All belong to God; the circle of love still includes them. This is what Charles Wesley declares in one of his great hymns:

> Outcasts of men, to you I call,
> Harlots and publicans and thieves!
> He spreads His arms to embrace you all;
> Sinners alone His grace receives.

God's love for us is so great that it includes judgment. It is a love which cares for us too profoundly not to chasten and discipline that a greater good may be found.

The love of God is not a dripping, sugary sentimentalism. It contains the strength of severity within it. It is necessary to declare this fact because the Hollywood version of love has corrupted it. In one sense it is a fearful thing to abide in the love of God.

There is no doubt that God's judgment operates in history and in personal lives; history is the story of God's judgments. Rebellion against God has brought fearful consequences on nations and societies. Under many of the tragedies which overtake individuals and families can be written: "The wages of sin is death" (Rom. 6:23).

In perceiving or experiencing the judgment of God many have seen it as a quality set over against the love of God. It has thus become a characteristic of God to be placated, changed. Often judgment has been presented as the moment when the love of God ceases and the wrath of God begins—as an ending of love.

The judgment of God is the love of God. It does not represent an exhaustion of the patience of God; nor does it express a change in the intention of God. It is still the love of God in action. As Nels Ferré says: "Holiness is love's negative work in relation to sin." Herbert Farmer makes a similar claim: "Man may sin himself into the judgment of God, but never out of his love."

Worthy human love is not without its severities and disciplines. A parent who indulges a child to the point that all restraint is absent does not love that child. True parental love yearns to see a child grow fine and clean and true. It would even prefer to see a child suffer in some degree if the alternative were that the child would live a life which is squalid and mean, even if it did include a shallow type of happiness.

Because God loves us in this profound—even tragic—sense, his judgments can fall upon us. But they are better called consequences than punishments. The most drastic of these consequences can still be called God's loving shock treatment for sin; for the purpose is health and wholeness and salvation. Again Nels Ferré is right when he says: "Justice is preparatory for love, for God always works to create and save."

Many an error in the thinking about the Cross would have been avoided had the unchanging nature of God's love been grasped. The hour of judgment is still the hour of love. God's love is expressed in judgment; it persists through judgment. The final word is spoken in the Bible in a score of places, as in the 107th psalm: "His [God's] mercy endureth for ever!"

"God so loved the world, that he gave . . . ." The nature of God's love is to act. God did not wait in some far-off heaven, witnessing passively the plight of his creatures. "For us men and our salvation" he plunged, in love, to our side. This is the fundamental "good news" of the Christian story.

There are few more significant passages in the Bible than the parable of the wicked husbandmen. (Mark 12: 1-11.) It is significant because of the revelation it gives of the self-consciousness of Jesus and, beyond his mind, of the mind of God. A man planted a vineyard and leased it to others. At the agreed time he sent servants to collect the rental. The first servant was ill treated. Later one was killed. Finally the vineyard owner sent his son. But the tenant said: "This is the heir; . . . let us kill him." And they did. They killed him and cast him out of the vineyard.

We would rightly question the reality of a love that stopped short of action. If a man were struggling for his life in the swift-moving current of a river and his friend merely stood on the bank shouting his affection to him, the quality of that affection would be rightly suspect. If God had merely sent messengers to tell of his love and nothing more, we would question that love.

The birth of Jesus means simply that God gave his best. He held back nothing. In giving him God came, not half-way, but all the way to meet us. In the cross of Jesus we know that God was ready to follow through to the bitter end.

There is an incident in the early history of Australia which perhaps throws some light on the nature and extent of the love of God. Samuel Leigh became the first Methodist missionary from England to faraway Australia. When he heard the call of God, he told his mother of his intentions. Naturally she was downcast, realizing that her son would be separated from her by months of dangerous sea travel and that probably she would never see him again.

In a few days, however, she accepted the sacrifice. When Samuel spoke to her again, she said: "Son Samuel, if the Lord called thee to be a missionary, He will no doubt enable me to give thee up."

Stripped of its theological complexities, is not this the type of love we see in God the Father in the gift of his Son, Jesus, to this world? As the parable we have quoted says: "Having yet therefore one son, his wellbeloved, he sent him also last unto them, saying, They will reverence my Son." God could go no farther; he gave his Son. Such is the love of God for us.

The love of God is an eternal love. It did not begin at Bethlehem, nor did it end at Calvary. The historic life and death and resurrection tell that which is eternally true. As Charles Dinsmore says: "There was a cross in the heart of God before there was one planted on the green hill outside Jerusalem."

Many a traveler passing in a ship along the coast of Italy has been awed by the volcanic activity of the island of Stromboli. All can be dull and quiet and dark. Suddenly from the bowels of the earth an eruption can develop. Molten lava pours down the mountainside and the hot ash is thrust into the night sky. An awe-inspiring glow fills the horizon. Stromboli tells of what is ever happening in the center of the earth. There great fires and molten rock surge and churn constantly. Only occasionally does the force that is there find a fault line and burst out, as at Stromboli. It tells of that which is true beneath.

The cross of Jesus tells of the love of God that always has burned for man. This is something of what the Bible says when it speaks of "The Lamb slain from the foundation of the world." It is a truth which is expressed in a modern poem by Leslie Weatherhead.

> I sometimes think about the cross,
> And shut my eyes and try to see
> The cruel nails and crown of thorns,
> And Jesus crucified for me.
>
> But even could I see Him die,
> I could but see a little part
> Of that great love, which like a fire,
> Is always burning in His heart.[2]

[2] From *A Plain Man Looks at the Cross* (Nashville: Abingdon Press, 1945). By permission of Abingdon Press and Independent Press, Ltd.

Why must anything come between God and his offered forgiveness? In a human family when a boy or a girl who may have committed a wrong comes to a father and asks forgiveness there is, if that repentance is sincere, a great readiness to pardon and to receive the erring member of the family back into its circle.

It is this universal, everlasting love of God which, according to Abelard, brings about our salvation. In the presence of so great a love we are humbled and ashamed. In its pure light we suddenly see ourselves. That which we see we do not like, and we bow in penitence. The love of God brings an answering love from our lives. As John says, "We love him, because he first loved us." (I John 4:19.)

Christian thinkers who have lived in the Abelard tradition have asked constantly a simple, probing question. In moral transformation what more is needed than repentance? If a sinner is moved to confession, God will forgive.

In Christ's best-known parable, the parable of the prodigal son, only repentance was needed to bring about the restoration of the son to the father's home. The prodigal son, by now in a far country, becomes repentant. "I will arise and go to my father, and will say unto him, Father, I have sinned against heaven, and before thee." (Luke 15:18.) It is enough. On arrival home his brave little speech of penitence remains uncompleted. At once he is forgiven and restored. No mediating acts are required; there is no time pause—nothing. The only condition of reconciliation is repentance. At once a father's love flows out to welcome and restore him.

The purpose of the Cross in the life of the sinner is to

bring forth repentance. As we see the length to which the love of God goes, as we grasp at Calvary some glimpse of its height and depth, we are subdued, convicted, and made ready for the transforming grace of God.

Love begets love. This is the essence of all types of Moral Influence theories of the Atonement. And who would deny the insight that is there? The love of God is eternal. The Cross did not change the mind and heart of God. Suffering love is the most powerful force in the universe. In its supreme expression in the Cross we bow our heads and examine our hearts. Through the doorway of penitence opened by the hand of love comes the forgiving, healing, transforming power of God.

Why has the main body of Christian thought, while accepting the Moral Influence interpretation of the many-sided cross of Jesus, declared it is not enough? Why has criticism been so heavy ever since it fell with primitive and unchristian severity on its first exponent, Abelard?

The basic problem of deformed human nature is how adequately to respond to love, even when it is seen. Sin is a fearful force which holds men and women in bondage. It spins its own deceptions. A sinner does not know the depth of his sin. How then can he repent for that which he does not fully comprehend? No man, of himself, can repent for all his sins. Even could he repent, does repentance give deliverance from a terrible bondage? Something more than the power of penitence is needed.

Then, too, the Moral Influence explanation of the cross of Jesus places a premium on gifted people. After all we are, each one, endowed differently. While every man is made in the image of God there are some who, through heredity and environment, seem to be able more easily to respond to God's appeal. Others are hardened and calloused by life. Repeated sin has made a response far more difficult.

Now if, in a sense, salvation comes through our response to the love of God revealed in the Cross, that salvation is more for the spiritually more-favored section of the human family.

Another complaint against the Abelardian view of the Cross is that it is far too subjective in its very nature to be adequate. It seems to say we are redeemed, not by what happens on the cross of Jesus, but by our response to it, by our feeling—reaction to it. As a result the Cross can easily be sentimentalized. The love of Christ at Calvary begets pity, and pity is an emotion which is altogether inadequate for the transformation of human nature.

By putting the emphasis on the response given to the Cross, we are really transposing the center of God's saving act from God himself to ourselves. It is our response which becomes all important. In the last analysis we are saved seemingly, not by Christ, but by our own emotional response.

Let me say at once that Christian discipleship does need objective reality. Some rock of salvation is needed on which we can knowingly stand. Our moods are too unreliable to be trusted. Our love, white hot during one day, can, so soon, burn down to ashes.

As Emil Brunner says in his book *The Mediator:*

All these inner moods and feelings, as they rise and fall, toss like the waves of the sea over an immovable sheet of rock, upon which these words are clearly inscribed: "I belong to Christ, in spite of everything, in spite of my moods and feelings, in spite of all my experience of my impotence, even in the sphere of faith. I belong to Christ, not because I believe in Him, but because of what Christ has said, through the Word which God has spoken to me in Him, the Mediator." [3]

It remained for James Denney to launch the heaviest of attacks upon this theory of the many-sided cross of Jesus. If the Cross only expresses a love which goes even to death, it is no more than a display of love. If there was no objective purpose in Christ's dying, then it merely parades the love of God. If there was no reason for dying, then why die?

Let us assume, if I may paraphrase Dr. Denney's argument, that two men are standing on a pier that juts out into the ocean. Presently one says to his friend: "I love you very much and to prove that love I am going to jump off this pier and drown myself." He does it, and next day the papers tell the story of the strange suicide of a man who for no purpose gave his life, so he said, for his friend. Let us imagine, however, that these two men are there again and one inadvertently trips and falls into the water. His friend, though a poor swimmer, plunges to his rescue and manages to push him toward a ladder of safety. In doing so he himself sinks and loses his life. Next day the papers in this case will tell the story of a hero who gave his life for

[3] (Philadelphia: The Westminster Press, 1947), p. 526.

his friend. The difference is that there was a purpose in the second dying; in the first there was none.[4]

If Jesus was merely giving a display of love, could it be described in any other term save—and we use it reverently —as the death of a suicide? Unless there was some objective purpose in dying it seems to have been without real reason. A display of love that is merely a display has no power; there is something artificial and shallow about it. It is when there is a real deliverance that comes through one's death for a friend that there is power in it all.

What is it Jesus accomplished by dying that could not be achieved by longer living? Was there any objective reality in his death on a cross? These are the abiding questions of all who wrestle with the meaning of the Cross. To them we must turn as we seek further to understand the many-sided cross of Jesus.

Nevertheless, let it be emphasized that whatever insights come, however far we go, we must never forget the centrality of the love of God. It remains our hope and salvation.

A story is told of Toyohiko Kagawa, the Japanese Christian leader, as he preached and worked in the slums of Toyko. A Western visitor to the city one day saw a small Japanese speaking on a street corner. To all who would listen he said: "God is love. Not love as you understand it. God is love, like Jesus."

Before we go further in life or in thought we face the Cross. Whatever else it is, it is the cross of God's love. Rus-

[4] James Denney, *The Death of Christ* (rev. ed., R. V. G. Tasker, ed.; London: Tyndale Press). Used by permission.

sell Maltby, the British theologian, bears a concluding and beautiful witness to the love of God in Christ. "On the Cross," says Dr. Maltby, "God betrothed Himself forever to the human race, for better for worse, for richer for poorer, in sickness and in health till death us do part." Yet even this is not enough. Even death does not bring the love of God to an end. "I am persuaded, that neither death, nor life, . . . shall be able to separate us from the love of God, which is in Christ Jesus our Lord." (Rom. 8:38, 39.)

CHAPTER III

The Central Mystery of the Cross

NO ONE CAN READ THE STORY OF JESUS WITHOUT BEING forced to conclude that he believed that by dying on the cross he was doing something which would not have been achieved by longer living. There pressed upon his mind some inner compulsion which kept him steadily on the way to Jerusalem. We see this conviction in such statements as the one in Mark 9:12: "It is written of the Son of man that he must suffer many things." Similarly in Matt. 20:28 appear the words: "The Son of man came not to be ministered unto, but to minister, and to give his life a ransom for many." Leslie Weatherhead expresses clearly an inescapable conclusion:

"The words of Jesus about His suffering and death reveal that he willingly committed himself to some mighty task,

costly to him beyond our imagining, but effecting for all men
a deliverance beyond their own power to achieve, and that in
doing so he knew himself to be utterly and completely one
with God the Father." [1]

What was this "something" which Jesus accomplished?
To ask this question is to move to the central mystery of
the many-sided cross of Jesus. To answer it in meaningful
words is to convey to others the mightiest of all God's acts
and to proclaim the very good news of the Christian faith.

Let me say now that I am convinced that there is "something" which Jesus achieved by dying and that the Christian disciple, no less than the professional theologian, must
go on searching for what it is.

Earlier in my ministry I could not have written so con-
fidently. The Cross as the revelation of God's love seemed
enough. Now I know it is not enough. Christian faith needs
the objective reality which the so-called "Work of Christ"
on the cross supplies. The love of God in Christ wins a
response from our hearts precisely because it was a real
deliverance he was winning for us. I may have to fall back
on an inadequate metaphor or on the language of poetry
to explain what Christ did for us. I only know that so to
believe puts a firm rock of salvation beneath my feet.

The story of Christian thought on the doctrine of the
Atonement is the effort to explain what it was Christ
achieved for us in dying. For two thousand years Christian
thinkers have struggled with this issue. From the very
earliest days of the church attempts were made to put into

[1] *A Plain Man Looks at The Cross, op. cit.,* p. 57.

words, into metaphors, into similes, this central mystery of the Cross. In surveying the thinking of the church on this all-important theme, one clear fact emerges. It is that the metaphors used and the doctrines fashioned in an effort to explain the meaning of the Cross have reflected the thought patterns and the cultural atmosphere of the period. For this reason it is hard for us who live in today's cultural pattern to fully understand just what the thinkers of another period were trying to express.

The idea of blood sacrifice was dominant in Jewish circles in the first century. Everyone knew what it meant to offer on the altar the animal of sacrifice. It was very natural then that the metaphor used in the first years of the Christian church was of sacrifice. In this thought form Christians tried first to express the truth of the Atonement.

The New Testament is full of sentences which hold up the death of Christ before the Jewish sacrificial system. Paul speaks in these terms: "[We are] now justified by his blood." (Rom. 5:9.) The Letter to the Hebrews declares it was necessary for Christ "to make reconciliation for the sins of the people" (Heb. 2:17). The apostle Peter understands the cross of Christ as sacrifice: "Forasmuch as ye know that ye were . . . redeemed . . . with the precious blood of Christ, as of a lamb without blemish and without spot" (I Pet. 1:18-19).

Throughout the history of the church ideas of sacrifice have persisted. Naturally, this has occurred because of the authority of the Bible and the place given to the Old Testament. Hence today's congregations of Christians still sing such hymns as the following by Isaac Watts:

> Not all the blood of beasts
> On Jewish altars slain
> Could give the guilty conscience peace
> Or wash away our stain.
>
> But Christ, the heavenly Lamb,
> Takes all our sins away;
> A sacrifice of nobler name,
> And richer blood than they.

Always, and especially in earlier days, metaphors drawn from the Jewish sacrificial system were full of meaning and gave glimpses into the significance of what Christ did for us all.

In the years when slavery was common to the world, the idea of Christ as a ransom given to set men free was used. For almost a thousand years the Atonement was expressed in terms of the slave system. Man was in bondage to the devil, and Christ paid the ransom price on the cross, as a slave might be set free through a ransom paid to his owner. This concept has a New Testament basis, for Christ himself described his death as a "ransom for many." Hence, there have always been those who have seen Christ as a ransom price, granting them freedom from the tyranny of sin.

During the Middle Ages feudalism was the system which men understood. It was the day when knights were brave and bold and rode the earth demanding satisfaction for slights given to their easily wounded pride. So it was that in those days there arose a theory of the Atonement which looked upon Christ as satisfying the hurt pride of God. Christ was then presented as our satisfaction. He removed the affront to God represented by sin, and forgiveness became possible.

Later still, the law court dominated the thinking of people. There were many more crimes on the statute books of a land like England than there are today. In England there were no less than 160 violations of the law which brought the death penalty. They included such crimes as these: to pick someone's pocket of more than one shilling, to grab goods from somebody's hand, to shop lift, to steal a sheep or snare a rabbit, to appear on a highway with a blackened face. As a result, the hanging of men, women, and children was commonplace. Charles Wesley mentions that he once preached to fifty-two people awaiting hanging, one a child ten years of age. Executions were public, and bodies—sometimes ten or fifteen at a time—were left rotting in chains for people to see. The hangings at Tyburn took place every six weeks, and people paid for seats to witness the executions.

Another sword which hung over the people's heads was being jailed for debt. Men were thrown into prison if in debt, and thus were unable to earn the money to discharge the debt. Jails were places of cruelty, bribery, and disease.

The pictures evoked in the minds of the people by the thought of a law court were vivid indeed. Many of them lived in constant fear of going to court. The Christian thinker and preacher, when he spoke of Christ's being a substitute for us, of his taking our place on the cross that we might go free, was using an understandable metaphor of great relevance and power. People understood when the message of the pulpit declared: Christ paid our debt, he died in our stead on the cross, he suffered our penalty.

> Bearing shame and scoffing rude,
> In my place condemned He stood;
> Sealed my pardon with His blood:
> Hallelujah! what a Saviour!
> —PHILIPP BLISS

Here then was a metaphor, belonging to the experience of the people, which after being picked up and baptized into the Christian faith, gave vivid glimpses into the meaning of Calvary.

The important fact to remember is that these metaphors and mental pictures of yesterday have largely lost their meaning today. Most people cannot think beyond their experience. No longer does the sacrificial system of Judaism remain a vivid part of our religious life. The slave market is gone. Feudalism is dead. Comparatively few people ever face a court of law; and with the expansion of justice, its terror is gone. To try to understand what Christ did for us by using these metaphors of the past involves an effort in understanding the metaphor itself before we penetrate to its inner meaning. Therefore, the time has come when, apart from their historical significance and the riches that they reveal as their historic setting is understood, these metaphors have largely lost their value. We must seek new ways of expressing what Christ did for us in the cultural pattern and common experiences that are appropriate to the midyears of the twentieth century.

In seeking a metaphor that is understandable in terms of

modern experience, some Christian thinkers have turned to the idea of Christ as a reconciler. Harold De Wolf of Boston University can be a spokesman for this attempt. In *A Theology for the Living Church* he says:

The idea of reconciliation has taken on continually richer connotation in recent times, due to such varied experiences as those of mediation in international and industrial disputes, of marital counseling and of psychiatry. . . . A view stressing change in personal attitudes and relations would seem to be better designated as a doctrine of reconciliation. This title has the additional advantage of employing the nearest English equivalent of a New Testament term employed several times in this connection.[2]

Reconciliation is costly. A Christian minister in counseling situations, a psychiatrist identifying himself with his patient, know the price to be paid through emotional empathy in being a reconciling agency in a broken personality. A marriage guidance counselor can tell of the same cost in trying to draw together a divided home. The Industrial Conciliation officers in Australian labor disputes pay the same price in mediating in the quarrels in industry. In international affairs the mediator, the reconciler, has become a familiar figure as he grapples with the issues of war and peace.

Here, then, is a picture that has meaning for us today. By grasping this metaphor we gain glimpses into truths that lie at the heart of the cross of Jesus. Through his death Christ was mediating between God and man. After

[2] (New York: Harper & Brothers, 1953), pp. 264-65.

all, one of Paul's greatest sentences makes just this claim: "God was in Christ, reconciling the world unto himself" (II Cor. 5:19).

There is another picture which is familiar to modern man. It is almost a symbol of our culture. It is the picture of a white-robed scientist poring over his instruments in a laboratory. For every one of us this is a real metaphor closely related to our own experience. Disease is dark and deep; its grip on life is real and frightening. It is the scientist who wrestles with his power of evil and carries on a lone battle on our behalf. It is a struggle that is not without risk. Many a scientist has himself suffered and died in an encounter with the dark forces of disease and death.

The scientist is a pioneer of the kingdom of health. Though he suffers, we, because of his suffering, are made whole. Yet the victories he achieves do not automatically flow out in blessing to us all. We must appropriate his triumph. To as many as receive the gift of his discoveries to them is given the power to know wholeness and health. Literally because of what the scientist does, many of us go free.

There are obvious weaknesses in the idea that Christ can be likened to a suffering scientist winning his lone battle on our behalf, conveying to us the benefits of his gains. There is the most obvious weakness that a scientific laboratory is largely an impersonal place, rather than an arena where human relationships must develop. The scientist handles things, whereas Christ offers his salvation to persons. Thus, there is an absence of personal encounter in the idea of Christ's Atonement being comparable to the victory of a scientist in his struggle against disease and death. Likewise, the gains of the scientist come in an impersonal way if we are ready to allow them to operate. Christian salvation can never be likened to a curative or preventive medicine. It is not something which, once received, operates mechanically or automatically in human personality. Always in relationship between Christ and his followers there is an intensely personal interaction. By faith, and faith alone, we must receive the salvation that is offered. Yet in spite of these limitations many of us may catch a glimpse of what Christ has done for us by seeing him as a suffering scientist.

Let me then develop the analogy of Jesus Christ not as a "suffering servant," as the prophet Isaiah depicted him, but as a "suffering scientist." In the various phases of the struggle we may catch some glimpse of what that "something" was that Christ accomplished for us on the cross of Calvary.

First of all, Christ, as is true of a research scientist, waged through his life, death, and resurrection a lone struggle with the powers of evil. As a white-robed scientist grapples with disease and death in a laboratory, sometimes at the risk of his own life, so Christ wrestled with sin, probing into its nature and robbing it of its power. Through his victory we find health and freedom.

Is there a power which can be called a kingdom of evil? Does evil exist outside individual lives? These are crucial questions. Certainly something outside the sin of individual lives seems to operate. Augustine perceived this fact long ago, describing the phenomenon as "an evil mass." J. S. Wale, the English theologian, says: "Your failure matches mine and our lives interlock to form an organic system of evil. There is in the world of our experience a kingdom of evil by which the evil acts of each individual are inspired, sustained and re-enforced." This suggests that the origin of evil is in individual hearts but that it can, when given expression, interlock with the evil rising from other lives and form a "sinful mass."

Some time ago I was present at a conference in which one of the senior statesmen of Australia was grappling with a most difficult national problem. In his opening remarks he revealed the sincere attitude of an idealist. He loved the people, he had his solutions. He could, I am convinced, have succeeded in his principled thinking if he had been able to have his way. After he spoke, however, the leaders of the contending elements in the dispute arose, one by one. Each with some passion gave forth a one-sided view, largely expressing selfish judgments. Slowly I watched that cabinet minister slump down in his seat. It seemed as if from the entrenched evil in the situation, from the bitterness and the selfishness, there came a heavy blanket whose folds closed around him, weighing him down. There was apparently no way through it. At last, defeated, the conference adjourned. Looking back I am sure I witnessed in that room the individual selfishness and evil of hundreds of lives coalescing, interlocking to make a matted undergrowth through which no pathway could be cut.

It is against this sinful mass, this kingdom of evil, this power of the demoniac that the New Testament presents

Jesus Christ as waging constant warfare. He, as a champion, contended against the forces of darkness. He sought their secret and tried to rob them of their power. He was triumphant. In his lone battle with evil he emerged as the victor.

I wonder if we can see this wrestling of Christ with the powers of darkness in terms of the scientist grappling with the powers of disease? Let me give an illustration.

There lived from 1857 to 1932 a man named Sir Ronald Ross. He played a major part in the great victory over malaria, a disease which had been the curse of man for centuries.

As far back as the fifth century B.C., Hippocrates had noted the relationship between marshy, swampy areas and the incidence of malaria. It was not until 1880, however, that a French physician, Charles Louis Alphonse Laveran, discovered the malarial parasite in human blood.

Ross was a doctor in the Indian medical service, and in 1892 he began studying malaria. He bred mosquitoes, feeding them on the blood of malarial cases in an effort to prove his theories. For two years he worked daily from eight o'clock in the morning until four in the afternoon. Often he became almost exhausted with the intensity of his fight. His microscope rusted from the perspiration of his hands. Day after day he searched, and always he had the same result—nothing. At last after long months of search, he isolated a malarial parasite in a mosquito, and he was able to discover and study the life cycle of this parasite. He had confirmed the hypothesis of Sir Patrick Manson: that the mosquito was the host of the malarial parasite at one stage of its existence, and therefore an active agent in its spread.

Ross later proved the transmission of bird malaria by the *culex* mosquito, and he applied the practice of mosquito destruction for the control of malaria. Still much remained to be done, but it was the beginning of the end for malaria.

As I think of a story such as this, which could be repeated many times in the history of medicine, I catch a glimpse of what Christ did for me. He grappled with the moral germ that we call sin. He wrestled with the powers of darkness. He pressed into the very citadel of the kingdom of evil, robbing wickedness of its dark secrets and power.

Secondly, in waging his ceaseless warfare against the powers of evil, Christ suffered and died as a casualty in the battle. As a suffering scientist may give his life for others, so Christ gave his life for us.

No one can doubt that a scientist pays a price for the gains he brings to his fellow men. I have always been deeply impressed with the magnificent story of Marie and Pierre Curie, the discoverers of radium. They believed there existed some element which no one had yet isolated or seen. They began their series of experiments with pitchblende, trying to isolate this new element. Knowing little about it, they were unaware of the risks they were facing. At last they succeeded. During one night, which they called "a night of wonder and magic," as they sat in the crude shed which was their laboratory, they watched the strange glowing of radium in the darkness.

These two dedicated scientists paid a price for their victory. For the rest of her days, Marie Curie carried in her twisted and deformed hands the evidence of the strange power of radium to inflict suffering on those who handle it unwisely. She died prematurely because of the radiation which she absorbed. These two became suffering scientists through the price they paid for their victory over ignorance and disease.

Christ in grappling with evil paid his price. That price was a cross on a lonely hill. We may well ask the question, "To whom was that price actually given?" For a thousand years men believed that the price was paid to the devil. Actually no one received the price. A social reformer pays a price for the advance he brings in human affairs. The road of progress has always been marked by the crosses of those who have dared to be ahead of their time. But the price is not paid to any particular person or being. The mother, we say, pays a price in her care of her children. The price is exacted but nobody receives it. The scientist pays a price for his loyalty to truth, for his integrity, his obedience to the research standards of his profession; but the price is paid to no one. So it is with Jesus Christ. It is not necessary to define who may have received the price. It is enough to say it was paid.

The third step in the analogy of Christ as a suffering scientist is that the battle he wins, the gains he offers, the results of the price he pays, must be received by us all, must be appropriated before they are of any use to us.

Here again our analogy holds. The day came in the battle against poliomyelitis when Dr. Jonas Salk found a vaccine that protected children and adults from the dread scourge. The vaccine was prepared and rushed to hospitals around the world. Great campaigns were launched to convince parents that every child should receive inoculation against polio. Yet all remained useless until there was an acceptance of the gains available, until there was a receiving into human bodies of the protective health that was now offered.

I can recall in my own ministry dealing with a family where polio had struck at a little girl. She lay paralyzed and helpless, facing months, perhaps years, of therapy. Never again would her wasted little limbs be as strong as they once were; always she would live the life of a partial cripple.

The chief tragedy was it could have all been avoided. How those parents condemned themselves! Healing was available in terms of preventive medicine but they had been too busy, too careless to appropriate the gains of the scientist's victory. And so that victory had remained external to the one they loved. She suffered, not because healing was unavailable, but because there had been no acceptance of its gifts into her own life, no appropriation of the victory that had been won.

Nothing happens automatically in the moral and spiritual world. Christ has won his victory, but it remains external to us—indeed for us it might as well not have happened—if we keep it outside our own lives. By repentance and faith the benefits of Christ's passion must be channeled into our lives. Only then do we receive the victory.

Any Christian who cares for people is often oppressed as he sees the consequences of the failure to appropriate the gifts Christ offers through his conquest of evil on the cross. Every minister knows what it is to cope with moral delinquency in a young man or a young woman. He knows all too well it was all unnecessary for such tragedy to have come upon the home, a personality, a community. Parents were too busy following their own affairs, too careless of the God who had created them and redeemed them to see that their children were surrounded by the power of prayer and worship. So they denied to their children the opportunity of receiving the redemption of Christ.

Take another example. A minister faces a woman who, in mid-life, is distraught and broken in personality. Neurotic tendencies have become uppermost, her personality is broken. Why? Selfish living, with emphasis on possessions, or money, or family. There has been no acceptance of the serenity that God offers in Christ. There has been no inner integration of personality that salvation can bring.

So it may be with our own lives. Some of us are suffering today from the exhaustion and defeat that we have encountered in our struggles with evil. We are going on our way, not appropriating the power available to us. Christ as a suffering scientist has died in vain as far as we are concerned. We have failed to lay hold of his promise and his power. Always in God's world there must be the opening of heart if the moral and spiritual power released by Christ are to flood into us. Only as this happens can it be said: "Christ died for our sins according to the scriptures."

Finally, Christ as a suffering scientist challenges us to live as he did. He challenges us to accept the quality of sacrifice and obedience which he revealed. As we are ready to make this response so our salvation becomes complete.

What stories there are from the annals of science concerning the devotion and the obedience of those who have labored on behalf of others for victory over disease! Many times there has been revealed a quality of integrity and patience and sacrifice which humbles us all. A tradition of service has been set up. The unbroken line of sacrifice for others has been kept. So the story of one scientist, risking all, giving his life for another, has brought a similar response in those who have come after him. This is the power the suffering scientist has had over the minds of his fellows.

During World War I, at a hospital at Neuilly in France, many soldiers were being brought in with deep shell wounds which were already infected with tetanus or gas gangrene. In that hospital, a doctor named Taylor suspected that this particular condition of the wound, which nearly always proved fatal, was caused by a specific bacillus. If that bacillus could be found, argued Dr. Taylor, a cure might be found.

Dr. Taylor began his many experiments with bacilli from the wounds, but it was always difficult to be sure that the right bacillus had been found. Final proof could only be supplied by inoculating a human being. Obviously, there was danger in such a course, for it was pressing out into the unknown.

In that hospital worked a young nurse named Mary Davies, who was a student of bacteriology. Knowing of

Dr. Taylor's dilemma, she inoculated herself with a preparation of the bacillus, went to bed, and sent a note to Dr. Taylor telling him what she had done. He immediately hurried to her side and injected the chemicals which he hoped would act as a remedy. For a day and a night the life of the nurse trembled in the balance as the infection raged in her body. Then Mary Davies was pronounced out of danger. Through her obedience to the highest ideals of her profession she played her part in a great victory which has brought healing to thousands.

Christ has always been able to draw from human hearts a quality of obedience which has changed the world. He who took up his cross has inspired many also to take up the cross and to follow him. Let it be emphasized that without this response there is no real salvation. Salvation is never an experience to be enjoyed alone; it is a challenge to be accepted. It is to take hold of the values, the spirit that caused Christ as a "suffering scientist" to risk his all for us and to translate them into our own life and experience. It is only when this is done that Christ's salvation is perfected in us.

CHAPTER IV

The Benefits of Christ's Passion

JESUS DIED FOR ME. RUNNING THROUGH CHRISTIAN experience and literature since the first century has been this simple conviction: Jesus died for me. So persistent is the claim that it demands an explanation. Why have men and women, at the foot of the cross, been so sure that in a very personal way the benefits of Christ's passion flowed out to them?

The belief that Jesus died for individual men and women arose at the very beginning of Christian history. It is written right across the New Testament: "Christ died for our sins according to the scriptures" (I Cor. 15:3).

Jesus himself first made the claim. "The Son of man came . . . to give his life a ransom for many." (Mark

10:45.) At the Last Supper, as he offered bread and wine, the symbols of his death, he said: "This is my blood . . . , which is shed for many" (Mark 14:24). In the writings of Paul, of Peter, of John and of the author of the Letter to the Hebrews the idea recurs on page after page: "His own self bare our sins in his own body on the tree" (I Pet. 2:24).

We might well ask, "How can the death of someone who died two thousand years ago affect us today?" To answer the problem of the time factor is relatively easy. Time, in great events, does not seem to matter. Think of some of the happenings of the past—the signing of the Magna Carta by King John at Runnymede in 1215; the nailing of his ninety-five theses to a church door in Wittenberg by Martin Luther in 1517; the sailing of the Mayflower in 1620. These events happened long ago, but they affect us all today. They were, in a sense, done "for us."

It is far more difficult, as we have seen, to define just what it was that Jesus did in dying "for us." It is bound up with the realization that sin is serious and forgiveness is costly. It recognizes that pardon cannot be offered or received lightly or cheaply.

Russell Maltby, in his little book *Christ and His Cross*, poses a fundamental issue. He says: "[The Cross] is the divine solution of what is always the problem of forgiveness, namely, how to make forgiveness utterly free without making it free-and-easy; to forgive the sinner without condoning the sin; to achieve reconciliation without compromise of the truth." [1]

Jesus, by bearing the burden of sin, by accepting in his own flesh the consequence of sin, subdues and humbles us. While we accept his forgiveness, it can never be done lightly, not before the background of the cross. Somehow, with deep moral significance, we are led into the experience of the unbelievable pardon of God.

For two thousand years the death of Jesus has been seen in terms of substitution. Difficult as are some of the problems related to substitutionary sacrifice, there is reality in the idea. Something rises from our hearts which gives spiritual significance to the hymn we sang as children:

> There was no other good enough
> To pay the price of sin,
> He only could unlock the gate
> Of heaven, and let us in.
> —C. F. ALEXANDER

When we use the phrase "Jesus died for me," there are two possible meanings. One meaning, already mentioned, is that Jesus died as substitute, "in our stead." The other interpretation says that Jesus died for us in the sense of dying as representative—"on behalf of us."

One of the most significant contributions of Christian thinking on the Atonement during this century has been the development of the idea of Christ as representative of man. Christ died "for us" as our representative, in accordance with the scriptures.

[1] New York: The Abingdon Press, 1936, p. 124.

What, then, does it mean to say Christ died as our representative? In what way did he stand in the presence of God on our behalf? If we could grasp something of this answer we would see another great truth which belongs to the many-sided cross of Jesus. "Christ died for our sins according to the scriptures."

Christ is our representative because he expresses for us our deepest yearnings, articulating that which we in our dumb way cannot voice.

There is a deep inadequacy in most lives, an inadequacy of expression. We just cannot put our feelings into words. There are desires and yearnings that remain cooped up within us and are never voiced. These feelings can be of love for another; they can be for a finer and truer life; they can be for God. More than we will ever admit, we "hunger and thirst after righteousness." Many of us scarcely recognize what it is that is struggling for expression within us; nor would we know how to give voice to it even if we knew what it was all about.

It is because of this "dumbness" that many of life's activities satisfy us. Music and drama of the highest kind grip us because they give voice to our souls. When we are enraptured by good music, when we are spellbound by some great dramatic presentation, we feel someone is saying for us that which we cannot say ourselves. Similarly, an act of worship, filled with the noble majestic cadence of the Bible verses, finely expressed prayers, the hymns of the church, and a moving sermon all carry us out beyond ourselves. We feel, before God, we have something with which we can be identified. Through it we approach the throne of God's grace.

In a similar way great men of history, great events interpret for us what is unvoiced within us. A noble man appears in history. He represents the best of his community. Somehow he gropes his way forward and taps unsuspected qualities within the lives of ordinary men and women. They follow him, and he is able—often after resistance from those who cannot see what he sees—to drag the whole of mankind after him. He comes to represent the highest and the best—which as yet is hidden—in human hearts.

The world's most noble statue to a great man has this effect on me—and I am sure on many others. In Washington, D.C., is the United States' tribute to Abraham Lincoln. He sits, carved in marble, towering above all who look up at him. There is the noble, rough-hewn face, its lines etched, as it were, by the sorrows of the war in which he was forced to play so crucial a role. Behind his head are engraved some of his noblest utterances. The immortal Gettysburg address is there. As I read those words and looked into the face of the greatest American of them all, I was elevated in spirit. He expressed a quality of selfless living, a vision of human justice, a spirit of greatness, which drew from somewhere in the depth of my being aspirations usually covered by life's lesser duties and interests.

I am sure you have felt like that in the presence of some people, of some incidents of history. You are lifted beyond yourself. You feel you are represented, the best that is you, in that one whom you love and admire.

It is significant how often it is that only in some crucial focusing of issues, some mighty struggle, some profound suffering, that the deepest yearnings of humanity are revealed. Through an act of self-sacrifice, through a price paid, we see the truth.

Hence the greatest moments of history have been drawn out of conflict. Suffering, sacrifice, death have become the occasion for the noblest expression of life. Socrates drinking the hemlock; Jesus on a cross; Stephen dying as a martyr; Joan of Arc perishing in the flames; Abraham Lincoln falling with an assassin's bullet in his brain—all had to die to be the truest and finest representatives of the human race.

I wonder, does all this explain what the Bible is saying when it declares Jesus died "for us"? He is our supreme representative. In him we see expressed what is deepest in our lives. He has a purity and a selflessness which tug at our hearts. He yearns to live close to God his Father. He shows a tenderness and a compassion toward his fellow men. And all these qualities are what we would long to express; yet we find it impossible to do so. We cannot even put into words, into intention, what we desire, let alone struggle for them.

Jesus does it all for us. He, in his life and death and resurrection, is the person we want to be. He draws to the surface of our lives the groping, unexpressed desires of the depths of our lives. Most of all, through his death does he reach us. There we see more of the wonder of his Spirit expressed than anywhere else. Thus the cross of Jesus, as the climax of his life, represents us at our truest and best.

"Christ died for our sins." He, on our behalf, reveals the hidden depths of our beings. He is our representative, expressing for us that which we in our inarticulate helplessness cannot express ourselves. In him our souls find their voice. On our behalf he speaks and lives. "Christ died for our sins according to the scriptures."

Christ is our representative in repentance. He, who knew no sin, is the only one who can gather up our penitence and truly confess our sins. "Christ died for our sins according to the scriptures."

The question is often asked: Why is it necessary for Jesus, or anyone else, to die for our sins? If God is our heavenly Father and we are ready to ask forgiveness, is that not enough? After all, as we have seen, that is the teaching of the parable of the prodigal son.

Why, then, is it not enough for you and me when we sin merely to repent? Why must someone else, some other action, come between us and God? Why should the Bible say: "Christ died for our sins"? What possible difference could Christ's death make? If we came to God saying humbly and honestly, "I have sinned," why was that not sufficient?

Here is a reply which I think is valid. We need Christ as our representative in repentance. We need someone who can express deeply and fully our penitence for us. As Vincent Taylor says: "At best our penitence is pitiful, partial and individualistic. It needs to expand its broken wings by resting upon a perfect penitence voiced by the Son of God." [2]

There is sense in this claim. After all, one of the characteristics of sin is its blinding power. "Sin," says Jacques Martineau, "is unique. The more we practice it, the less we know of its nature." Sin weaves its own cloak of deception. As a result, every sinner suffers from a measure of self-deception. It renders us incapable of truly repenting. We just do not know how deeply we are involved in sin, and therefore we cannot fully repent of our sin. Emil Brunner puts his finger on the crux of the problem: "If we could repent as we should no Atonement would be needed, for then repentance would be atonement." We cannot repent as we should. It never, never goes deep enough. Therefore, we in our own strength can never receive the full and needed measure of the pardon of God.

There is only one who could fully repent, and that would be one who has never sinned. Only a sinless man knows the true nature of sin. There was only one sinless man who ever lived, and his name was Jesus. He saw the nature and consequence of sin in all its starkness. He was thus able to gather up all the horror man should feel at sin, all the yearning after complete purity and righteousness. He alone could repent for us.

And this is what Jesus did—and what Jesus does. He is our representative in repentance. There was a deep and wonderful meaning in his words from the cross: "Father, forgive them; for they know not what they do." It is literally true of all of us. None of us—anywhere, any-

[2] *The Cross of Christ, op. cit.*, p. 96.

time—know what we do. But Christ knows. And knowing, he expresses in identification with us his penitence. He is our representative before God. He gathers up our sin and becomes our spokesman in confession. "Father, forgive them; for they know not what they do."

There is a most significant illustration of the principle of vicarious repentance in the postwar experience of the church in Germany. When Martin Niemöller at last came from Hitler's prison, two facts confronted him. He discovered the depth of Germany's wickedness, especially in the treatment given to the Jews. He saw, for example, the white-painted board erected in Dachau concentration camp. It read: "Here between the years 1933 and 1945, 238,756 human beings were incinerated." The second impression which pressed itself upon him was the moral complacency of the German people in the face of these appalling facts. Hiding beneath others' sins, the people felt no condemnation, showed no guilt, because of the sins they felt their enemies had committed.

Gradually a great resolve formed itself in Niemöller's mind. He would lead his people in a national act of penitence. So it was, when the first conference of Christians assembled after the war, Pastor Niemöller preached the opening sermon. He chose as his text Jer. 14:17-22. "Therefore thou shalt say this word unto them; Let mine eyes run down with tears night and day."

Out of that conference came a historic statement. It was called a Declaration of Guilt. In it the Christian leaders said: "We say with great sorrow: through us endless suffering has been brought to many peoples and lands

.... we accuse ourselves of not having borne witness more courageously, not having prayed more faithfully, believed more joyously and loved with greater ardour." [3]

For two years Pastor Niemöller made the burden of his message the "Declaration of Guilt." Among the German people he aroused a bitter resentment. They called him a traitor to admit guilt before the world. People walked out of churches where he spoke; students boycotted him, staging marches of protest in places where he went.

How right was Pastor Niemöller. Above all things Germany—and every nation—needed to repent. Yet if any man was free from guilt in all Germany it was Martin Niemöller. As he said: "True, I had an alibi in my pocket for the years 1937 to 1945, my identity disc from the concentration camp."

So the man who in one sense was most free from guilt alone felt the guilt. He saw the nature of sin. He repented, for himself and for his people. He became a representative in repentance. So many of those who carried a greater guilt knew not what they did. Sin had blinded them, stopping repentance.

We stand today—all of us—as sinners. None of us knows the range and depth of the sin in which we are involved. So, like the German people, we justify ourselves. We avoid the shame of our own sins by criticizing the sins of our neighbors. We have no deep sense of the need for confession and pardon.

[3] From *Pastor Niemöller* by Dietmar Schmidt. Copyright © 1959 by Dietmar Schmidt. Reprinted by permission of Doubleday & Co., Inc. and Odhams Press.

How desperately we need the Christ. How we need to
accept him as our representative. How we need to have
him as our Saviour to go into the presence of God saying:
"Father, forgive them." Only then shall we find forgiveness. In our helplessness we are unable to find pardon in
our strength. Christ is given for people just like us. He is
our representative. He confesses our sin and thereby makes
it possible for us to be pardoned. "If we confess our sins,
he is faithful and just to forgive us our sins." (I John
1:9.) Only Christ can confess for us. "Christ died for our
sins according to the scriptures."

Christ as our representative mediates for us a new relationship. In a deep and wonderful sense he becomes our
spokesman before God and out of it comes the life of reconciliation.

There are many situations in our modern life where
we trust to a representative to be our spokesman and
mediator. He, acting for us, does what we could not do
for ourselves. It is done in a court of law. We choose a
lawyer to plead our case. The deeper the trouble we are
in, the more we want a lawyer, one who understands the
situation, who can negotiate for us. We do it in labor
union affairs. Every trade union has its elected representatives who mediate, and are the spokesmen for all the
members. We do it in political life. We send our representatives to Congress to conduct, on our behalf, the business of the nation. We do it in international affairs. Our
representatives go to international conferences, seeking
peace in the name of all the people.

There are times when the cost of being a representative

is high. It was so with Count Bernadotte, the Swedish mediator. In the name of United Nations, in the name of all humanity, he sought to intercede in the Middle East, to mediate peace. As he pursued his selfless task, hatred swirled around him. Grasping the issues involved, he led the warring nations toward peace. Then the evil hatred of the area boiled over and destroyed Count Bernadotte. He died, a representative of us all. Out of it came an awareness of the contending forces and of the nature of the struggle. Out of his death came shame. It played its part in bringing at least a measure of peace and a negotiated relationship. He, by his death, on behalf of us all, brought peace to us all. In a sense the Swedish nobleman died for our sin, the sin of the war-crazed human family.

The New Testament suggests often that Christ is our advocate, our mediator, our representative spokesman. This idea is very clearly expressed by John: "If any man sin, we have an advocate with the Father, Jesus Christ the righteous." (I John 2:1.) The same idea is found in the Epistle to the Hebrews. "For Christ is . . . entered . . . into heaven itself, now to appear in the presence of God for us." (9:24.) In carrying out this great ministry for us, Jesus died. He paid the final sacrifice on our behalf. "Christ died for our sins according to the scriptures."

Perhaps we imagine we do not need an advocate, Jesus Christ the righteous. We can do it all ourselves. Yet I wonder sometimes whether that is not one of the basic errors of our time. We imagine we can burst into God's presence at any time. We think we can practically skip up to God, seeking pardon, and have him forgive us, for "that is his business."

Somehow I think all who, in early centuries, treated evil as far more serious in God's sight were nearer the truth. When we are at the depth of our moral need we cannot lift our shamed heads. We know then we desperately need to have an advocate. We are grateful there is a representative, someone who can speak for us.

There is an incident in the life of John Wesley which, I think, illustrates what I am trying to say. A man named John Lancaster and nine of his companions were lying in prison awaiting execution. While waiting the dread day of death they were visited daily by a Methodist woman, Sarah Peters, who pointed them to God. The day came when "the jail delivery" set out, ten men journeying to die. As they trundled through the streets of London on the way to Tyburn they sang one of Charles Wesley's hymns. I can imagine that desperate scene. Men with no hope, condemned to death, had hope—hope in Christ. So they sang:

> Lamb of God, whose dying love
> We now recall to mind,
> Send the answer from above,
> And let us mercy find;
> Think on us, who think on Thee;
> And every struggling soul release;
> O remember Calvary,
> And bid us go in peace!

In the hour of deepest need, they looked away to Christ who was advocate and representative.

All I know is that this miracle has happened, does happen, and can happen to you and me. As we choose Jesus as our representative, as we put our trust in him, the peace of God comes. We are, through him, reconciled to God. "Christ died for our sins according to the scriptures."

Christ as Victim and Victor

IF WE ARE TO UNDERSTAND THE CROSS OF JESUS WE MUST possess, as it were, a bifocal vision. By this I mean two worlds are involved and both must be constantly kept in view by lifting our eyes from one to the other if we are to see the death of Christ in the wholeness of its significance. It is a cross of man, for men planned and crucified Jesus. It is an intense human drama, and we know the names of the principal figures in the tragedy. Pilate and Judas and Caiaphas and Peter all carry responsibility for the Cross. It is on the other hand far more than a human drama; it is the cross of God, of "the Lamb slain from the foundation of the world" (Rev. 13:8). Calvary is the mightiest of God's mighty acts. It is the instrument of our redemption, "God was in Christ, reconciling the world unto himself."

There is an interpretation of events given in the Bible which, at this point, we should grasp. It is that God is able to take hold of evil happenings, of tragedies, and turn the tables on them, transfigure them. He cannot alter that which has occurred, but he can lay hold of it, bringing good out of evil. Sometimes he does this so amazingly that we fall into the error of thinking God must have intended it all.

The cross of Jesus is a transfigured cross. God did not condemn his Son to death. God so loved the world that he gave his only begotten Son. It was men—men like you and me—who took hold of that Son and killed him. As we have seen, this is clearly the teaching of the parable of the wicked husbandmen: The father said, "They will reverence my son. But when the husbandmen saw the son, they said among themselves, This is the heir; come, let us kill him." (Matt. 21:37-38.)

Once the Crucifixion occurred, God took hold of it. He did not intend it, but once it happened, God's alternate will, as it were, came into operation. God seized upon the Cross and, through his sovereign power, made it the occasion of salvation. As the Bible says: "The wrath of man shall praise thee." (Ps. 76:10.) The same truth is expressed in Eph. 4:8: "He led captivity captive."

As a consequence, the cross of Jesus is transformed. The crown of thorns, pressed upon the forehead of Jesus, becomes a crown of pearls. The gibbet on which Jesus died becomes a throne from which he reigns. The place of defeat becomes the scene of God's greatest victory. Christ reigns from the tree.

In his life, death, and resurrection, Jesus Christ was both victim and victor. Both must be understood if the meaning of the many-sided Cross is to draw upon us.

Jesus was a victim of human injustice and wickedness. His trial and death made up one of the great miscarriages of justice of all history. If we leave the godward side of his ministry out of the picture completely, we have left a tremendous drama in which good and evil, principle and expediency, sacrifice and self-interest, adventurous thinking and conservatism, love and hate meet. In the struggle that developed, Christ perished—a victim to the unworthy forces that operate in human hearts and human society.

What was it that crucified Jesus Christ? Who was it killed him? The Pharisees, the religious leaders of Jewish society, crucified Christ. It is a disturbing thought that it was the most respectable people of Jerusalem—the people who were the backbone of the worship of the synagogue, the people who were the puritans of the day, the people striving desperately to conserve the finest values of their heritage—who hounded Jesus to death.

The Sadducees, who were virtually the commercial leaders of the day, appear in the story. Commercial privilege was theirs, and seeing it threatened, they were ready to commit the crime of the cross. Rather than see any interference with their profits they were ready to manipulate the death of Jesus.

A government representative takes his dread place in the gallery of those who destroyed Jesus. Pilate tried his best to avoid condemning Jesus. He went to elaborate precautions to absolve himself of blame—even washing his hands in public to show it was not his decision to send Jesus to the cross. It is surely one of the ironies of history that the man who washed his hands of Jesus is the only one who has been named in the Apostles' Creed as being linked with Christ's death. Over the centuries millions have repeated: ". . . crucified under Pontius Pilate."

Herod, a gay, sensual, sophisticated man of the world, was one of those who silenced Jesus. Then there was Judas, who for greed and envy betrayed his Master, becoming perhaps the most infamous man of history. For thirty pieces of silver—the price of a slave—Judas shared in the tragedy. Amid it all there is the anonymous crowd that shouted, "Crucify him"—a crowd, its standards lowered by mass psychology and interested mainly in "bread and circuses," that carried Jesus toward death. The fickle Jerusalem mob, maneuvered by propaganda and slogans, bears responsibility. Roman soldiers played their part in the Crucifixion. They claimed it was none of their business, for their only task was to obey the orders of their superiors. They were using the age-old excuse of soldiers—passing over the control of their consciences to others.

To list the names of all who planned and carried out the crucifixion of Jesus is to catch glimpses into the pressures that challenge Christians of every generation. Henry Sloane Coffin, in his book *The Meaning of the Cross*, lists succinctly the forces which are at work to defeat the purposes of God. They are: "Religious intolerance, commercial privilege, political expediency, pleasure-loving irresponsibility, unfaithfulness, the mob spirit, militarism, public apathy." [1]

The drama that ended with the Crucifixion uncovers conflict on a deeper level between Jesus and the particular pressure groups of the period. It shows why Jesus is in danger of becoming a victim to evil in every society.

Christ is ever in peril, because Christianity, the world's only incarnational faith, challenges men in every phase of their living. Therefore, it comes into conflict with men in relation to the things which they care most about.

Jesus died because he dared to enter Jerusalem. He perished because he challenged the centers of religious, commercial, and political power. If Jesus had been content to remain in Galilee on the circumference of human affairs, he would probably have been ignored, remaining virtually unmolested to the end of his life.

By entering Jerusalem, the center of Jewish civilization and the local imperial power of the Roman Empire, Jesus was challenging the life of the times at its heart. He declared, by his very presence and by such acts as the clearing of the temple of the money-changers, that all life was his concern. Nothing escaped the sovereignty of his truth. Economic, cultural, religious, and political affairs were subjected to God's authority and power. This was the claim inherent in Christ's appearance in Jerusalem.

Within a few days of Christ's journey from the circumference to the center of the nation's life, groups who felt their power challenged were meeting together in huddled

[1] (New York: Charles Scribner's Sons, 1959.)

corners, planning his death. They wanted him either to keep quiet or go home to Nazareth. Because he would do neither they crucified him.

I am convinced that one of the most frequent and vital conflicts in all generations and every type of society is between Christ and those who would keep him far from Jerusalem. The world tolerates a religion which functions as a specialized activity, following its own rites and ceremonies but being silent before the paramount interests of men and women as they live out their daily life. The world by one means or another always tries to silence a religion which will not "stay in its own backyard."

A vivid modern example of one of the world's most crucial and continuing conflicts comes from the clash between Hitler and the Confessional Church in Germany. In his biography, *Pastor Niemöller,* Dietmar Schmidt describes the gathering struggle between Christian forces led by Martin Niemöller and the Nazi state. The day came when Martin Niemöller and his colleagues were summoned before Hitler. In the midst of the conference Hitler was provoked to declare: "You confine yourself to the Church. I'll take care of the German people!" In other words, he was declaring clearly the attitude of his regime to the church. He had no objection to the church's continuing its quite pastoral ministry—baptizing, marrying, burying. Indeed, Hitler's government continued paying traditional church subsidies until his death. A church criticizing public policy, protesting against the ruthless extermination of the Jews, resisting state control of church affairs was a different proposition. Such a church had to be silenced.

Before the interview in Berlin ended, Martin Niemöller sealed his own fate. As each man filed past Hitler, shaking his hand, Niemöller, with great courage, made his protest, carefully choosing his words: *"Herr Reichskanzler,* you said just now: 'I will take care of the German people.' But we too, as Christians and churchmen, have a responsibility towards the German people. That responsibility was entrusted to us by God, and neither you nor anyone in the world has the power to take it from us." [2] This statement led to the day when Niemöller became Hitler's personal prisoner, continuing so for eight years, scarcely escaping with his life. A church challenging the central places of power could not be tolerated.

We have no need to go back even twenty years to see at work the forces which made Jesus their victim in first-century Palestine. The evils we have named are perennial ones, deep-seated in human nature and in the very structure of human society. The outward appearance of society may change from feudalism to capitalism, socialism to Communism, but the same power-struggles are there and the same forces are waiting to crush anyone who would interfere with privilege and power.

American—and world—society saw during 1959 a further vivid illustration of the fact that the forces which crucified Jesus Christ are operative in our own day. What was the whole mean story of rigged television programs but a story of the crucifixion of truth and decency and

[2] Schmidt, *op. cit.,* pp. 93, 94.

honor? For the sake of money, power, and prestige men were gradually cajoled into perpetrating a colossal fraud. A deep shame has come to countless people because men they thought could be trusted had betrayed them.

In a sense, however, we should have expected it. This is the kind of onslaught that evil perennially launches against men and human society. Yesterday it was the slaveowners and the industrial exploiters who could not be trusted; today it is the manipulators of the modern mass-mind who have proved their unworthiness.

Mankind today faces a new peril, the control of human nature through the manipulation of mind and emotions. With the world's attention fixed on atomic research and outer space, the startling advances in the understanding and control of human personality are being almost overlooked. Actually, the sciences which deal with human behavior have been advancing as fast as the physical sciences.

As Peter Drucker points out in *Landmarks of Tomorrow,* "Science has almost reached the stage where man can be treated as a biological machine, controlled by the manipulation of thoughts and emotions. The great peril of the nineteenth century was the exploitation of man for industrial purposes, the growing evil of the twentieth century is the increasing manipulation of the people." [3]

The manipulation of man has been seen in its most diabolical form in the techniques of brainwashing. In lesser ways it also appears through research advertising, subliminal advertising, and the blanket pressures that can

[3] (New York: Harper & Brothers, 1959.)

be exerted through television and the other mass media. Unfortunately the technique of the big lie and the little lie often repeated has been learned all too well.

So it is that in new settings Christ goes on his way to Calvary. In the vivid light of an ancient tragedy we see ourselves and our society. The value of the story of the cross of Jesus is that it uncovers forever the power and nature of evil. It sets clanging a bell, warning us obviously of the dangers ahead and around us always. One of the great contributions of the many-sided cross of Jesus is that it shows us Christ as victim. In seeing him as victim, crushed by the evil forces of his day, we see the perils of our own hearts and our own times.

The victim becomes the victor. Bad Friday becomes Good Friday. The triumph of the Cross is vindicated in the victory of the Resurrection.

Throughout these pages we have insisted that the cross of Jesus should not be seen in isolation. The Cross was the climax of the life, and it must be viewed in relation to all that went before. It must also be linked with that which came after, the resurrection of Jesus. The many-sided cross of Jesus is a cross of victory.

Gustaf Aulén of Lund in Sweden is responsible for a re-emphasis on the so-called "classical tradition" of the meaning of the cross of Jesus. In 1930 he was invited to give the Olaus Petri lectures. They were later published and then translated into English with the title: *Christus Victor*.

It was the forward-looking aspect of the Cross which gripped the thought and imagination of Professor Aulén.

Aware of the power of evil he saw the Cross as a lone battle between the forces of evil and the Christ; and when the struggle was over, the victory remained with Christ. It was this victory which for him was the central fact of the Cross.

Let Aulén speak for himself:

The Atonement is set forth as the Divine victory over the powers that held men in bondage. The Divine love prevails over the wrath, the blessing overcomes the curse by way of Divine self-oblation and sacrifice. The redeeming work of Christ shows how much the Atonement "costs" God. For my own part, I am persuaded that no form of Christian teaching has any future before it except such can keep steadily in view the reality of the evil in the world and go out to meet the evil with a battle song of triumph. Therefore, I believe that the classic idea of the Atonement and of Christianity is coming back—that is to say the genuine authentic Christian Faith.[4]

In the first century and with the early Christians the victory of Christ on the cross was all-important. There was, in those days, a vivid belief in the power of evil, in the mythology of the period evil spirits roamed the earth, all too often controlling the lives of people. Paul speaks of this conviction when he talks of "principalities and powers in heavenly places." The hierarchy of the demoniac was understood in some detail. It was believed, for example, that there were seven layers of air between earth and heaven. In each of these levels a different species of evil

---

[4] (New York: The Macmillan Co.), pp. 162-63. Used by permission of The Macmillan Company and S.P.C.K.

spirits lived. At intervals these demons plunged down to earth taking into bondage individuals, even whole communities of people. As a consequence, Professor Ramsey says that people in the first century were suffering from "a failure of nerve."

Into a world groaning under the power and the tyranny of evil Christ came. He was sent to do battle with the power of evil. The whole life, death, and resurrection of Jesus was seen as the most crucial moral and spiritual encounter of all history.

Jesus was introduced to the world by John the Baptist in these terms: "Behold the Lamb of God, which taketh away the sin of the world!" (John 1:29). When Christ commenced his ministry, he at once went into the wilderness, and we are given the tremendous encounter of the temptations. There he battled with evil. When it was over the devil left him; but the account adds significantly, "for a season." The struggle, with an initial victory to Christ, was only beginning. The vast struggle mounted in intensity until Christ entered the Garden of Gethsemane. There so profound and bitter was the conflict that he sweat great drops of blood. Then came the Cross itself.

The cross of Jesus, although it seemed a victory for evil, was far more. It was the occasion of the final triumph of Christ. Presently the great cry was heard: "It is finished." Jesus did not say: "I am finished." "It is finished" was the cry. It was a declaration of victory. Here is the *Christus Victor*. Then came the postscript to the cross of Jesus— the Easter story. The Resurrection underlined, verified the victory which the Spirit of Christ had already won at

Calvary. As men saw him radiant and transfigured outside the empty tomb they knew that the forces of evil had gone down to defeat. Christ was truly victorious.

What does it mean that Christ was victorious over evil? It means that in the most crucial battle between right and wrong of all history Christ defeated evil. In him goodness at its best and evil at its worst met. When the battle was over the victory was his. The early Christians grasped the significance of it all. The demons in the sky, the evil spirits which roamed the earth had met their match. Christ had conquered. As a consequence Paul could sing his great song of triumph: "[God,] according to the working of his mighty power, which he wrought in Christ, when he raised him from the dead, and set him at his own right hand in the heavenly places, far above all principality, and power, and might, and dominion, . . . hath put all things under his feet."

The victory of Christ has tremendous relevance to our own times. We have lived through a period when the world has been rediscovering the power of evil. It was not so long ago that a supreme optimism prevailed, and evil seemed soon to be left behind in the onward march of mankind.

Suddenly the evil man thought was subsiding erupted with frightening, devastating consequences. World War I marked the beginning of decades of evil. Drenched by war, startled and shamed by cruelty, men knew not how to explain what had happened nor did they know where to turn.

In it all the thought-world of the first century seemed

very near to our own. Our mythologies are different. We do not imagine demons inhabiting the sky above us, but we have learned afresh of the reality of "principalities and powers." We saw evil forces under the Nazis in Germany take hold of a whole nation, turning it to the ways of ruthlessness and war. We have seen the demoniac at work in certain aspects of communism, in the rise of McCarthyism in America, and in the spreading influence of the liquor and gambling forces of modern society.

Justice Jackson, speaking at the Nuremberg war trials, mentioned the effects of the resurgence of evil. "No such half century has ever witnessed such a slaughter on such a scale, such cruelties, such annihilations, such wholesale deportations and annihilations of minorities. These are the overshadowing facts by which generations to come will remember these decades."

Such a world needs: *Christus Victor*. The message of the Christ who through his cross and resurrection overthrew the hosts of evil is a startlingly relevant message. Amid our kind of world it "speaks to our condition," as the Quaker George Fox would say.

We might well ask, of course, that if Christ conquered evil why is there so much of it still in the world. It is a question not easily answered. I wonder, however, whether a metaphor will help. Oscar Cullman, in his book *Christ and Time,* points out that a war is won not through its final battle but by some crucial struggle much earlier in the conflict. So, it can be argued, the issue of World War I was really decided in the Batle of the Marne. In World War II victory was won at Stalingrad or on the beaches of

Normandy. From then on Hitler was a defeated foe. He still possessed sufficient strength to lunge out and hurt and kill and destroy. But the issue had been decided. In the midst of the conflict the victory was won.

In the encounter between Christ and the forces of evil at Calvary the most crucial conflict of all time was waged. When it was over Christ was victorious. Evil still possesses tremendous power. It still holds men in bondage; it still destroys. But evil has met its match. We know now it is only the second strongest force in the universe. Christ is victorious. Hence the Christian today is able to sing:

> O love of God! O sin of man!
> In this dread act your strength is tried;
> And victory remains with love;
> For Thou, our Lord, art crucified!

The significance of the victory of Christ in the midst of the years was brought home to me at the great First Assembly of the World Council of Churches, held at Amsterdam in Holland in 1948. The accent of the dominant European delegation was something of a puzzle to one who came from the far southland of Australia. Gradually however the truth dawned. The European Christians had been face to face with the stark and terrible nature of evil. At times they could do no other than cling to the faith that Christ, on the cross, had defeated the powers of evil. No wonder, then, they wanted to sing again and again a hymn of resurrection, making it virtually the theme song of the Assembly. I can still hear the fervor and the gladness which were there as they sang of a newly proved faith.

Thine be the glory, risen, conquering Son,
Endless is the victory Thou o'er death hast won;
Angels in bright raiment rolled the stone away,
Kept the folded grave-clothes, where Thy body lay.

Thine be the glory, risen conquering Son,
Endless is the victory Thou o'er death hast won.[5]

In one Holy Week during Martin Niemöller's long imprisonment under Hitler, he noticed during his exercise period at Sachsenhausen concentration camp a word scratched on the path. It had been placed there by another Christian minister, Heinrich Gruber, who was also a prisoner. On the gravel was the word: *"Vivit—He lives."*

The meaning of the many-sided cross of Jesus must include the glorious message of the Resurrection. *Vivit*—He lives! *Christus Victor!*

[5] Hymn by E. L. Budry; trans. R. B. Hoyle. Used by permission of The Epworth Press.

CHAPTER VI

The Cross of Identification

TWO CROSSES STAND UPON THE PAGES OF THE NEW TESTA-
ment and in Christian history. The first cross belongs to
Jesus alone. By dying he does something for us which we
could not do for ourselves. As we watch him going out to
die, he moves away beyond any other event in history.
We find it impossible to follow him, even in thought. As
we watch him, we know our attitude can only be one of
adoring gratitude. Christ is winning a lone victory, achiev-
ing a lone salvation "for us men and for our salvation."
All we can do is to bow before the terrible isolation and
loneliness of the Cross, reaching out groping, grateful
hands to accept the benefits of his passion. As we have already seen, there is the central cross at Calvary on which
the Son of God is dying. This cross is Christ's alone.

Yet there is another cross standing on that green hill beyond the walls of ancient Jerusalem which can be called "everybody's Calvary." It is the cross each one of us is invited to share—the cross of identification. This second cross, which belongs to us all, is not so clearly delineated as the cross which belongs to Christ alone. It is there, however; and if we look for it in the New Testament and in Christian experience we shall find it. It is toward this second cross that we now look.

The first glimpse we have of the cross of identification is on the road to Jerusalem. At the end of two years of ministry Jesus decided that he must go to Jerusalem. His disciples protested because of the risks involved. Jesus admitted the danger but pushed on, challenging his men to go with him. He said, "Whosoever will come after me, let him deny himself, and take up his cross, and follow me." (Mark 8:34.)

A little farther along that road to Jerusalem, Jesus spoke again of his coming suffering and death at Jerusalem. James and John asked Jesus to give them special, preferential privileges when he came to power in his kingdom. Jesus said: "Ye know not what ye ask: can ye drink of the cup that I drink of? and be baptized with the baptism that I am baptized with? And they said unto him, We can. And Jesus said unto them, Ye shall indeed drink of the cup that I drink of; and with the baptism that I am baptized withal shall ye be baptized." (Mark 10:38-39.)

Everybody's Calvary rises clearly in the Garden of Gethsemane. Jesus took his three disciples, Peter, James and John, into the garden amidst the old gnarled olive trees. Presently he said to them: "Sit ye here, while I go

and pray yonder." Twice he returned to find the disciples
asleep and said: "What, could ye not watch with me one
hour? Watch and pray." Coming to them a third time and
finding them again asleep, he said: "Sleep on now and
take your rest: behold, the hour is at hand, and the
Son of man is betrayed into the hands of sinners. Rise,
let us be going." (Matt. 26:36-46.)

What is the meaning of this moving request to remain
alert with him in Gethsemane? Is he asking that his men
should act as sentinels, warning him when those who
would betray and arrest him were at hand? I suggest that
this would be a shallow interpretation of a great hour. He
was inviting them to share that last hour of freedom with
him. He yearned that they should be identified with him
in his spirit's struggle as he grappled in the darkness with
the issues of his coming death. He was inviting them to
share his lonely vigil, being one with him in its tension
and its sorrow.

We see everybody's Calvary outlined most clearly as we
look back upon the cross of Jesus through the eyes of Paul
and Peter and the later writers of the New Testament.
Running through Paul's whole thinking is the amazing
truth which he discovered: that he, Paul, was able to share
in the cross of Jesus. It can be seen in Phil. 3:10: "That I
may know him, and the power of his resurrection, and
the fellowship of his sufferings." Peter, too, reflects the
same idea as recorded in I Pet. 4:13: "Rejoice, inasmuch
as ye are partakers of Christ's sufferings."

The most vivid sentence in the Bible, and one which
uncovers the outline of everybody's Calvary, is in Col.

1:23, 24, where Paul says: "I Paul, . . . now rejoice in my sufferings for you, and fill up . . . the afflictions of Christ in my flesh." The great Greek scholar, Joseph Lightfoot, has paraphrased this sentence of Paul in a manner which brings out clearly its inner meaning. Dr. Lightfoot says: "Yes, I Paul, the persecutor, I, Paul, the feeble and sinful, am permitted to supplement—I do not shrink from the word—to supplement the afflictions of Christ. Despite all that he underwent, he the Master, has left something still for me to undergo. And so my flesh is privileged to suffer for his body—his spiritual body, the Church."

The many-sided cross of Jesus includes a cross of identification. In the deepest sense we, who may follow Jesus Christ, are invited to share in his suffering. The very redemptive purposes of God are not entirely closed to us. We are challenged to go his way, seeking his goals and his triumphs.

What is involved in accepting everybody's Calvary? In the deepest devotional and religious sense, to what ministry are we called if we are willing to go the way of the cross? How does this great principle of identification which Christ places before us work itself out in our lives and in our own times? These are questions to which we must seek an answer.

First of all, when we are invited to "fill up the afflictions of Christ in our flesh," we are being called to the way of service and sacrifice. The chosen method of the Kingdom, a method which applied to Christ and which applies to us, is that of suffering love.

In the tremendous struggles in the wilderness at the beginning of the ministry of Jesus, the issue was clearly defined. There, in the forty days of testing, Jesus virtually chose the manner of his ministry. In three successive temptations, Jesus faced one fundamental issue: whether he would go the way of power or the way of service. In the first temptation Jesus looked on the possibility of turning stones into bread, of showing his control of the world and of using it to meet the physical needs of men. In the second he was taken to the Temple in Jerusalem and in imagination he saw himself as a wonder-worker. Again it was the temptation to overawe men with power. In the third temptation he stood before the sword and felt the fascination men have always felt for taking the way of naked force. Underneath each temptation, however, was a single issue concerning the nature of his coming ministry. Had Jesus succumbed to any one of the three temptations he would have chosen to seek a position of supremacy over his fellows. He would have set out to overawe and to win allegiance by authority and power. Jesus rejected them all and chose to become a humble servant of God and man. He decided that the way of the cross, the way of suffering love, was to be his way. In humble obedience and sacrifice he set out to face the tasks of his ministry.

Bruce Kenrick, in his book *The New Humanity*, declares that to be a Christian, to be a follower of Jesus, is to accept a similar way of service and sacrifice. He relates Christ's insight to the mission of his church, the mission of Christ's disciples in all generations. Let me quote Dr. Kenrick's words:

Jesus expressed the nature of their mission in one luminous sentence—"As my Father hath sent me, even so send I you." He had been sent to identify himself unreservedly with men, to share their sorrows, their griefs, their sufferings; to penetrate into the depths of their lives, to be wounded, to bleed and to die. That was how the Father had sent him. And now—"so send I you." [1]

The world, including even that of the Christian church, has found it almost impossible to follow Jesus in his acceptance of the Cross. So deeply ingrained is our desire for power—whether it be in politics, international affairs, or the life of the church—we cannot imagine that there can be advance through servantship. Far more readily than we are willing to admit do we accept the Führer concept; and far more than we ever admit do we admire the man who takes the way of authority and power, lording it over his fellows. This is why a Hitler and a Stalin become accepted by millions of people. To so many of us it seems right that the principle of leadership, of authority, of power is the right principle.

The Führer principle has often corrupted the church. The whole conception of the hierarchy of some of the great churches of the world is a departure from the simplicity of Jesus and the way of service and sacrifice that he followed. I read a phrase recently concerning a leader of one of the churches of the world: "He was a great prince of the church." One would have thought the very association of the concept of prince with a follower of

---

[1] Used by permission of Wm. Collins Sons & Co., Ltd.

Jesus would have been offensive to the point of blasphemy. How strange it is that a follower of the lowly Jesus is referred to as "my Lord," as is accepted with the bishops of the Church of England. The Führer principle has penetrated great sections of the church. The church, through history, has revealed too many men who found pleasure in the conscious exercise of unconscious power.

The same departure from the way of the cross has brought judgment upon some Christian missions. In the nineteenth century the missionary cause of the church took and planted the Christian cause in the uttermost parts of the earth. It moved outward at a period of colonial expansion in the political life of the Western world. It undoubtedly carried with it not only the Christian message but some of the overtones of its cultural and political period. As a consequence, the principle of leadership rather than the principle of service sometimes expressed itself. The missionary, in spite of his attempts to avoid it, often established a form of lordship over the primitive peoples. Now, of course, history has changed.

In this twentieth century any form of tutelage is unacceptable to so-called backward peoples. Where the church has made friends with the men of power, it has suffered the setback that they have suffered. In countries such as China overseas leadership of the Christian church has been virtually banished, and it will be long years before the continuing indigenous church will overtake the unfortunate impression it has given to people that the Führer principle rather than the service principle operated within it.

The principle of service and of sacrifice always gives the church its power in witness. Again let me quote some creative words from Bruce Kenrick:

Until Christ crucified takes on visible form the world will not believe. "Except I shall see in his hands the print of the nails and put my finger in the print of the nails . . . I will not believe," said Thomas to Jesus. This is precisely what the world says to the Church. We who talk of walking the way of the cross dare not show men our hands. For we have not been wounded for them, we have not suffered for them. We have done little more than preach for them. When the world sees as well as hears—when the world sees, as it were, the print of the nails in our hands, then the world will have seen not only us but our Lord. And men will echo the confession of Thomas, "My Lord and my God." [2]

Secondly, the acceptance of the cross of identification means that we must be ready to move out to the lonely places of Christian witness. Only as we are willing to move toward the frontier with Christ shall we truly serve him.

Henry Sloane Coffin has pointed out that there are, in another sense, two types of crosses at Calvary. On two of them, on either side of Jesus, were dying men who had fallen below the standards of their day. As thieves and murderers they had flouted the accepted moral code of their period; so they suffered and died. On the central cross, also dying, was Jesus, who had risen above the standards of society round about him. The reward which society gave to all three was the same—a cross. It is to the

[2] *Ibid.*, p. 90.

cross of Jesus, the cross that awaits those who push on ahead of their time, that the Christian is called.

What tremendous power lies in the pressures for conformity? These pressures always harshly bear down on the mind and life of the man or the woman who deviates far from that which is accepted. In our time, however, the forces of conformity have been immensely strengthened. The power of the mass media, the fear of Communism, the upheavals of our time, have all turned this age into an age of conformity. We see it in young people. Orthodoxy is admired; the radical is suspect. This generation of young people is the most quiescent and conforming group of young people of the century. All of us are most cautious about what we say or do.

It should be obvious to us, however, that there can be no advance in any field of life save through nonconformity. Life always goes on as it is if there are no bold and brave men who step out from the mass of people, accepting the risks of the lonelier frontier posts of their time. It is to such lonely places that we are called by the Christ who himself died in the advance, probing line of the battlefield of history.

After all, the moral and spiritual world can be likened to a vast battlefield divided into three areas. There exists, fortunately, territory which already belongs to Christ. Painfully and slowly it has been won through the centuries and the gains have been consolidated. Then there is a far larger area firmly held by "the enemy." Within this territory Christ's authority is almost unknown. Between these two areas is a no man's land over which, in ceaseless warfare, rages the struggle between Christ and antichrist. In this struggle, and ever pushing forward, is the thin advance guard of the Christian forces. For those who belong to it there is constant danger—danger of becoming isolated, danger from the sniper, danger of death. In every generation someone must march to the lonely outposts of the kingdom of God.

There is a simple test which everyone of us, I think, might apply to ourselves. Are we, if we accept Christian discipleship, living at the frontier? If we say nothing more than a sub-Christian society would on great issues such as peace and war, racialism and economic structure, we might well ask whether we have found that frontier. We might also wonder whether we have found the frontier if we are mere reflectors of our own segment of the human family. If you and I—if we live in the West—think no differently about the events of our time than does our Western culture, we might again ask whether we have discerned the boundary of the kingdom of heaven. We can go even farther and ask whether we are conforming to the values of our era of history. Every generation creates its own mental climate which falls like a blanket over the mind of the entire human race for a period of time. Thus, if in our thinking we conform to the general attitudes of mankind as a whole, we may ask again whether we are expressing our citizenship of God's realm.

We must be realistic. To move to the Christian frontier is to move toward danger. History bears frequent witness to what is involved. Society has been very consistent in its persecution of those who have dared to lead it. Suffering is not far away from all who will not conform, all who are ahead of their time.

One of the great British preachers of the last century was the Rev. F. W. Robertson of Brighton. Very early in his life he found fame as a Christian leader. He was a prophet far ahead of his time. Gradually, as the quality of his thinking and leadership became more apparent, the crowd that had earlier flocked around him began to criticize. There came the time when he realized the strength of the opposition he had aroused. In the face of mounting criticism he wrote in his diary: "I shall be left alone as my Master was. I am hated by some who loved me once, not for what I do, but for what I think. I have long foreseen it. And knowing that the Father is with me, I am not afraid to be alone though to a man not ungently made there is some sharpness in the thought."

If we accept the cross which belongs to every man it means we must be ready to take the lonely advanced places of Christian witness. We must move to the frontier with Christ. It is part of the price of going the way of the cross, of accepting "everybody's Calvary."

Thirdly, to accept the challenge of everybody's Calvary is to accept the closest identification with those we would serve and save. It is to press near to those whom we would serve, proving our oneness with them.

Long before Jesus came, the prophet Isaiah spoke of the coming deliverer whom God would send. With great insight he spoke of him as one who would be completely identified with man. The Suffering Servant, when he came, would be "numbered with the transgressors." He would "bear the sin of many." He would "make his grave with the wicked."

In due time Jesus came, and if there is anything that is true of his life it is that he followed a ministry of identification. He began his ministry by submitting to John the Baptist's immersion in the River Jordan. He who knew no sin himself accepted oneness with sinful humanity at the very beginning of his public life. Throughout his ministry he crossed the class and caste lines of his time. He made friends with publicans and sinners. So closely did he consort with them that presently his enemies sneeringly said, "He is a friend of sinners." In this statement we can read the nasty innuendo which has come down through the centuries: "Birds of a feather flock together." Presently his identification was so close that they said not "He is a friend of sinners," but "He is a sinner." So close did he press to the sin of Jerusalem that in the end it broke not only his body but his heart. He went down into the loneliness and isolation of man's severance from God. How else can we understand the great cry of dereliction at Calvary: "My God, why hast thou forsaken me?" In his voluntary acceptance of solidarity with mankind he shared the very separation from God which is the chief consequence of sin. He suffered a criminal's trial and died a criminal's death. Our last picture of him is of a crucifixion between two thieves. He was literally numbered with the transgressors. He made his grave with the wicked. His identification was complete.

Jesus became identified with the least and the lowest and the lost. If I can say it reverently, Jesus was a "social climber," but of a different variety than those we know. We ever seek to climb upward, aspiring to the social group above us. Jesus climbed downward, identifying himself with those lower down on the social ladder, but nonetheless people in need.

In our modern society Christian identification is largely absent. In our Western society today a Christian is rather the acme of respectability. He is the exponent of conventional morality. He is the wearer of neat clothes. He is the sound and safe member of society. He is one of the chief props of the established order of things. In one sense all this is eminently right. Yet should a Christian be sound and safe in a world of horror and need? Should he be quiescent in a world undoubtedly filled with suffering and injustice? Should he not so identify himself with those in desperate want that fighting for them and with them he becomes one of society's turbulent and disturbing figures? Should he not under certain circumstances be numbered, as was his Master, with the transgressors?

Let me talk to myself for a moment and to no other. I find life good and wholesome. I have a home, a wife I love, children I adore, work which is rich with interest, friends who give constant loyalty. I am far away in pleasant Australia—away from the destruction of war and the pitiable hunger of our time. Food is plentiful and good. I sleep soundly most nights. Yet in a world like this should any man sleep soundly at night? Should I not be awakened constantly by the cry of starving children on the streets of Shanghai and Calcutta? Should I not feel the sorrows of war, which for so many millions are by no means past? Should I not remember vividly the seared and broken people of Hiroshima and those who carry still in their bodies and in their minds the torment of prisoner-of-war camps? Should I not feel the grinding wheels of poverty which still crush so many in the slums of London, New York, and Sydney? In a word, should not the conscience of the Christian today be a tortured conscience, painful enough to drive one to unceasing action?

You may say, of course, that to carry the sorrows of many in this fashion would be morbid and useless—would it? Without the bearing of sin voluntarily, there will be no bearing of it away. Until men the world over become so conscience-stricken at the thought of war and poverty and famine that they can no longer live with themselves, these evils will remain. To spring to action, to struggle to overcome these evils would involve us in action which would earn the condemnation of our less Christian contemporaries. It could be that we would be confused, as Jesus was, with the sin we try to remove. Could it be that this is what, in part, it means to be a Christian?

Some years ago I read the words of a Christian socialist. I forget his name, but his words deserve repetition: "While there is a lower class, I am in it. While there is a criminal element, I am of it. While there is a soul in prison, I am not free." That is the spirit of one who has pressed near to the cross we are all invited to share, who has accepted a place in the redemptive purposes of God.

The way of identification is the way to human hearts. Let us be brave enough and devoted enough to take the cross of identification to ourselves, and we shall see the answer of men. Then it will be we shall find them asking questions such as those quoted by Dr. Kenrick: "Why do these men come down and dwell amongst us? Why do they give us of their substance and their life? Why do they share our sorrows and our burdens? Why do they bind up our wounds with such compassion? Why do they weep when we are weeping? Why do they mourn when we are mourning? Do they want to be crucified? Like Christ?" [3]

The Russian novelist Dostoevski says somewhere, "Love in practice is a harsh and terrible thing compared with love in dreams. It is for love in practice that the world waits."

There is a moral truth which I think can almost be proved. It is that human progress waits for men who will step across from privilege and identify themselves with those who need help, fighting for and with them. It almost seems as though evil is so exhausting that those who are its victims have no power left to throw off the shackles which hold them in bondage. Thus God must wait for men and women who, not exhausted by the evil against which they would grapple, are able to come to it with freshness and power and to bring deliverance to the captives.

It is surely significant that Abraham Lincoln and William Wilberforce, who never in their lives felt the crack of a slaveowner's whip across their bare shoulders, became the great liberators of the slaves; that Lord Shaftes-

[3] *Ibid.*, p. 91.

bury, the aristocratic member of the British House of Lords who had never crawled a chimney when he was a child or worked in a factory or a mine, battled for the establishment of justice in the mines and factories of England; that Albert Schweitzer, who is no victim of the darkness and the disease of Africa, struggles to lift the burdens from the bending backs of the African people. Above it all, Jesus himself, who was not exhausted by sin or blinded by evil, stepped down among us and set us free. God seems to wait for men and women who will voluntarily accept the way of identification.

There is a fine story which stems from the early days of the Salvation Army in England. One day a Salvation Army lass was arrested in Manchester for "obstructing the King's traffic." In other words, she held an open-air meeting, preaching the gospel of Jesus. In due time she came before the Magistrate's Court, charged with an offense. As the case began, suddenly there stood to his feet in the courtroom one of England's greatest barristers, Frank Crossley. He asked permission to share in the case, to fight the cause of the Salvation Army girl in the dock. Permission was granted, and the great Frank Crossley crossed the floor and took his place by the girl, fighting back for her. It was said that the atmosphere was electric that day in the Manchester Court when a man of privilege quietly said he too was a Salvation Army officer and wished to be identified with one who was in need of a champion.

So we may pray:

Saviour divine,
Who perpetually for suffering humanity,
Dost bear the burden,
The dread relentless burden of redemption,
We pray thee that we thy servants today,
May, with these weak hands,
Uplift a little corner of the weight,
Which bears on thee.[4]

Fourthly, we can also say that those who accept the cross of identification receive the triumph which goes with that cross. It is a triumph that lies on the other side of suffering and defeat, but it is victory just the same.

We have been speaking thus far of the liabilities which belong to the cross of Jesus. They are there, and are severe and constant. But with the liabilities go the assets of the cross. As Vincent Taylor emphasizes: "He who goes down into the darkness with Christ shall also rise with him." The theme of the New Testament is this—no Cross, no Resurrection. If, however, there is a cross in any human situation there will most certainly be a resurrection. The hour will come when the power of God stands revealed. The moral universe remains always true to itself.

Suffering love is the most powerful force in the universe. We have lived through a period where brute force has been dominant. Two great wars, the violence of the dictators, the seemingly irresistible power of atom and hydrogen weapons, have all mesmerized us to a degree. We have almost come to believe that the only protection

[4] From *Prayers for Use in an Indian College* by J. S. Hoyland. Used by permission of W. Heffer & Sons Ltd.

is force, the only final arbitrament belongs to naked power.

All this is wrong. The greatest power among men is still suffering love. This is why where there is a cross there is always a resurrection. Where we offer God a cross of identification, he in turn hands us back an identification with the resurrection of Jesus and with the power of God which made the Resurrection possible.

Let us have another look at the story of Jesus. We see him at the end of his life standing in the judgment hall, alone. His disciples have deserted him. The crowds that had earlier flocked around him in gay approval have shouted: "Crucify him." Arrayed against him is all the might of the conservative forces of the Jewish nation and all the strength of imperial Rome. Against it all he stands with a crown of thorns on his head and a reed in his hand. His only weapon is a silly little reed.

Yet look what happened! This helpless Christ with a reed in his hand sent Peter out into the night weeping bitterly. This Christ plunged Judas into a remorse so terrible that, unable to live with himself any longer, he went out and hanged himself. This Christ, with no weapon save suffering love, drew Joseph of Arimathea out of his policy of safety first and caused him to beg for the body of Jesus and then to carry it, the body of a discredited prophet, openly through the streets of Jerusalem. This Christ caused the Roman centurion who stood at the foot of the cross to bow his head and say, "Truly this man was a son of God" (Mark 15:39). It was Christ who launched the infant church on its unpredictable course through the world. The power of the crucified Christ, with only a silly little reed in his hand and armed with his chosen weapon of suffering love, was irresistible.

There is one great fact to remember. It is that the spiritual world is consistent. Jesus said: "Do men gather grapes of thorns, or figs of thistles?" (Matt. 7:16.) The answer is No. But grapes do grow on grape vines and figs do grow on fig trees. Therefore, if the spirit that was in Jesus is revealed in us the same fruits of the spirit appear. If we are ready to take the way of service and sacrifice we shall know the triumphs that lie on the other side of service and sacrifice. The measure of our sacrifice, of our identification with others, determines the quality of the power that our life shall reveal. There may be no resurrection without a cross, but given the cross, be it our cross or Christ's, there will most surely be around it the resurrection power.

It is to the way of identification that we are called. Let me finish with a story. In the year 1580 a Dutch Protestant leader named Klaes was arrested and condemned as a heretic, and later burned at the stake. When the tragedy was over we might have seen, late that evening, Soetken, the widow of the dead man, taking her small son out through the back streets of the town to the side of a hill where their loved one had died as a Christian martyr. When she reached the place of execution she took from her pocket a small sachet. Stooping down, she gathered together a few of the ashes that remained. Placing them in the small sachet she tied it around her boy's neck saying simply: "My son, I place these ashes on your heart and on the heart of every son of these Netherlands in all eternity. Whenever and wherever in this world there is an injustice or wrong committed these ashes will beat on your heart and you will speak out without fear, even at the fear of death."

Here is the challenge which the cross of identification as part of the many-sided cross of Jesus brings to us. It calls us to take from the cross which belongs to Jesus the attitudes, the values, which made that cross what it is. To be a follower of Jesus is to press those values close to our lives. As we are ready to go the way of the cross, as we are ready to accept identification with Christ on his cross, so the power of God shall be released among men. It is a staggering thought. We are invited to share in the redemptive purposes of God. The call of the New Testament comes to you and to me: "I Paul, . . . fill up . . . the afflictions of Christ in my flesh." In the place of Paul's name we may place our own. "I, John; I, Jean; I, David; I, Mary . . . fill up the afflictions of Christ in my flesh."

Index